IF YOU CAN KEEP IT

A Constitutional Roadmap
To Environmental Security

Michael Diamond

6/96

Dear Tony,

Many thanks for your support – a wind under my sometimes tired + subluxated wings.

Yours

Michael Diamond

BRASS RING PRESS

Printed in the United States of America using soy-based ink and 50 per cent recycled acid-free paper.

First Edition

Library of Congress Catalogue Card Number: 96-83905

ISBN (Paperback): 0-9651309-0-8

Cover drawing by Frank Lacano
Cover designed by The Ad Agency, Inc.

*This book is dedicated to us all—
victims of environmental
domestic violence.*

ACKNOWLEDGMENTS

This work could not have been completed without the patience and understanding of my wife, Harriet, my daughters, Ellen and Linda, my mother, Ruth Brief, and my father, William Diamond.

Research and writing of *If You Can Keep It*, from its earliest conceptualization to the date of publication, spanned a period in excess of ten years. During that time, the project was kept alive by the kindness and encouragement of so many fine people. With apologies to those left out by a faulty memory, I wish to thank Bob DeMaria, Don Rudy, Al Porro, Michael Siegel, Elisabeth Scharlatt, Gail Rosenberg, Bill Evans, Ella Filippone, Rev. Gerald A. Pisani, Jr., Nancy Neuman, Dee Sadauskas, Jim Meyers, Walter Bjorkman, Jerry Mische, Jack Walsh, Richard Barbuto, Jean Wilhelm, Sr. Terri MacKenzie, Marcus Kantz, Rev. Franklin E. Vilas, Javad Tavakoli, Richard and Jane Cicchetti, Sr. Miriam MacGillis, Rev. Thomas Berry, Dick and Nancy Weber, Dominick Villane, Pat Bramwell, Denise and Neil Decker, Ana Kosok, Helen Chase, Clemente Toglia, Christina Durbak, Alex Hall, Megan McWilliams, Kirkpatrick Sale, Anthony Carusone, Pat Bramwell, Reid Shaw, Frank and Chris Wall, Marianne Williams, Joe Mikulka, Edison Wong, Barbara Hertz, and Sr. Nancy Fromelt.

John MacConnell did more than just work painstakingly with the manuscript. He served as a role model for me. I know of no one who walks this Earth so lightly and with such respect for nature.

CONTENTS

PREFACE

Much has transpired from the first Earth Day in 1970 to the final years of this century. The plight of the Earth has become quite generally recognized. The realization that as the Earth goes, so go we has also become well understood. The number of willing hands to help make things right, however, remains small. There is a reason for that anomaly; too few of us have seen a path that will actually lead to environmental security. In fact, most thoughtful observers have simply given up all hope of ever finding the way.

The purpose of this book is to shed light on a path that we can all take to environmental security. As with most "discoveries," this new path was there all along. We just overlooked it. In fact, it is a wide vista and was right there for all to see in, of all places, the Constitution of the United States. This book is meant to guide us to that new road. *If You Can Keep It* is meant to be a primer for a people's movement as we all take that fine road to health and safety.

CHAPTER 1

INTRODUCTIONS

If You Can Keep It is about the "domestic violence" clause in Article IV, Section 4 of the United States Constitution and how it can be used to get us through the environmental crises that we have brought upon ourselves. The clause has been sitting idle and unknown to the public for over two hundred years. During that period, our primary focus has been on rights: the right to vote and speak freely, property and privacy rights, to bear arms and have religious freedom, to name just a few. While the emphasis on rights is laudable, rights are only one side of a coin, the other side of which is responsibilities. The long forgotten "domestic violence" clause in Article IV, Section 4 is about *responsibilities*. I have become convinced that attaining security from environmental threats is impossible without our use of that clause.

It is with pleasure, therefore, that I make this introduction of the domestic violence clause to its owners–you, the American people. This long overdue meeting is both necessary and urgent. We've gotten ourselves into a perilous environmental situation. If the men who wrote the Constitution were here now, they would characterize the clause as a roadmap that they left for us in a time capsule. They had an abiding knowledge that, in the end, we would turn out to be our own worst enemy. They were correct. That clause was designed to get us back to safety and security.

You will find it in your copy of the Constitution following Articles I through III, which create, respectively, the legislative, the executive, and the judicial branches of the U. S. government. The complete text of Article IV, Section 4 is as follows:

> The United States shall guarantee to every state in this union a republican form of government, and shall protect each of them against invasion; and on application of the legislature, or the executive (when the legislature cannot be convened) against domestic violence.

In brief, Article IV, Section 4 requires the United States to *protect* us against *invasion* and against *domestic violence*. The former is the harm that other nations might do to us; the latter is the harm we're likely to inflict on ourselves. Our perilous environmental circumstances constitute a condition of domestic violence under the Constitution of the United States. The purpose of this book is to explore how your survival and the well-being of your children depend on that road map left in a time capsule by the framers.

A few introductory remarks about how I define environmental harms will be helpful to you. I view environmental harms as the man-made vectors or agents that bring about or contribute to death, disease, ill health, diminution of human potential, or damage to property. The vectors can be direct or indirect, but are always multiple and bring about harm in ways that are beyond our capacity to measure or easily comprehend.

The easiest environmental vector of harm to understand is one person causing a direct and known injury to another. For example, a farmer who sends a field worker out to use dangerous chemicals without instructions or protective gear commits direct environmental harm to that field worker. An indirect environmental harm occurs when the worker's child is born with a neurological deficit owing to the parent's exposure. The child's impairment or diminution of human potential will be made worse by the effects of additional multiple exposures to toxic materials in his own environment. Impairment often helps to bring about criminal and antisocial behavior, the effects of which are quite real and harmful, although difficult now to trace back to exposure of the field worker by the farmer. Well beyond the simple norms of proof upon which we base our reality, the child's problems are judged to be his own because the causative connection is beyond our capacity to measure or acknowledge.

If we consider the above example to be one web of environmental harm, picture the world as containing an immense and uncountable number of such webs all at the same time. They interact with one another in dizzying complexity, as when an entire population is burdened by certain toxic materials as well as being subject to local conditions. In addition to troublesome exposures in air, water, food, and consumer products, unnecessarily dangerous medicines and unhealthful nutrition choices combine to bring about inexorable declines in human health and human potential. To all of this burden, never before experienced by man, add the effects of global changes which are now becoming apparent. They include increases in ultraviolet radiation and carbon dioxide, a concomitant decrease in oxygen, global climate changes, and destruction of ecosystems upon which an ever increasing population relies for sustenance. These are the webs of morbidity that we have woven for ourselves. Together, they are what I define as our present condition of environmental harm–our present condition of environmental domestic violence as envisioned by Article IV, Section 4 of the U. S. Constitution.

It is an effort for me to keep in mind the definition of environmental harms as being, at the same time, direct, indirect, multiple, beyond measure, and interacting vectors of damage. I urge you to undertake the same effort. Only when we stretch ourselves to understand the vast nature of a problem can we get anywhere near to the solution. Theoretical physicist, Richard Feynman, devoted his life to original thinking in order to arrive at solutions. He would have us stretch our imaginations "to the utmost, not as in fiction, to imagine things which are not really there, but just to comprehend those things which *are* there."[1]

Continuing with introductions, I have been researching and writing about environmental matters since 1982. In 1981, I was employed as an environmental enforcement official at a state government department devoted to environmental protection. Although I saw and worked with some of the most competent people I have ever known, I understood even at a glance that the legal system we set up to protect us was woefully inadequate. Since then, I have been doing independent research to find a better way to handle environmental protection. That search led to the domestic violence clause. It was itching to be found and appears ready to be both studied and harnessed for serious environmental work.

Now, something about the readers. The vast majority of you care deeply about the environment. Having little or no experience with environmental laws, you may tend to believe that additional enforcement of them will make you safe. You are likely to take comfort from the sound of statutes like "The Superfund," "The Clean Air Act," and "The Safe Drinking Water Act." Those of you who have had direct experience with our environmental laws and the regulatory system are more likely to understand that those laws are grossly inadequate. However, not seeing an alternative, you address yourselves to those laws somewhat fatalistically in environmental organizations, businesses, government, and in academic pursuits.

Many of you are educators, health care professionals, criminal justice professionals, and employers. You do not yet perceive the connection between your worst problems and the environmental crisis. It is the purpose of this book to help you make the connection so that you can participate in solutions through the domestic violence clause.

I have spoken to many teachers who have been in the field for as long as thirty years. Without exception, they describe significant declines in student performance over that period of time. They are not surprised to learn the part that environmental harms have played. The institutions in which teachers are trained and in which they work, however, have difficulty accepting the fact that they must play a hands-on role in environmental protection. Environmental harms are a major driving factor in educational decline that won't go away unless and until confronted by educators *and* educational institutions.

In the course of my legal career, I've had much opportunity to work with people in the criminal justice system, from the judiciary to the police and all through the penal system. The connection between environmental harms and criminality is so palpable that I recognized it easily on seeing recidivists over thirty years ago. Just as alcohol impairs the ability to postpone gratification and comport oneself in accordance with legal standards, so do toxins, and people are now burdened with toxins in amounts that are wildly beyond our ge-

4

netic experience. If you are in the criminal justice system and want to stop the escalation of violence, you need to be involved in a hands-on way with environmental protection. You need to know more about the domestic violence clause.

Health care professionals–the doctors, hospital staff, dieticians, etc.–have been back-benchers, just watching an array of ineffective environmental laws allow the buildup of toxins within us beyond our genetic potential. In addition, those health care professionals have quietly watched the public's loss of biological wisdom in food habits,[2] without weighing in on the side of sanity. Worse, many modern medicines and procedures tend to be powerful and unnecessary vectors of ill health in-and-of-themselves. I have met with a number of young physicians who decry how tenaciously their medical societies and professional boards hold them to the use of such wasteful and harmful medicines and procedures. The rate of chronic illness in this country is increasing, not decreasing, while more and more money is being put into the present health care system every year. An understanding of environmental harms and the domestic violence clause can help to put health care professionals in the forefront of those who will be curbing ills that should not have befallen society in the first place.

I have met with employers, as well. They, like teachers, talk about a decline in worker capability and motivation over the last thirty years. Impairment is the rule, rather than the exception, and that is true in the ranks of both line employees and managers. An understanding of both the concept of environmental harm and the remedy of the domestic violence clause has the potential to bring employers and employees together in ways never before dreamed possible. The common enemy is our own lack of good judgment about the environment. Our errors and our shortsightedness must be corrected rather quickly.

I've saved the most crucial introduction for last. The vast majority of Americans do not truly comprehend the type of country that we've become. Continual drumbeating of propaganda and plaudits of self congratulations tell us that we are the cradle of democracy and the hope of the world. In fact, we are not that at all. In a permanent state of war since 1946, we now lack the vision necessary to maintain democratic institutions and to be a force for world peace. As such, we will continue to squander our public monies and our available resources on preparations for war. Devoting resources to protecting ourselves against environmental harms is likely to be little emphasized. The domestic violence clause is the much needed Constitutional counterweight to this nation's over-indulgence in the ways of war.

James Madison warned that "a standing military force with an overgrown executive will not long be safe companions to liberty. The means of defense against foreign danger have been always the instruments of tyranny at home."[3] The tyranny now being practiced in our country that threatens our liberty is the military use of the great bulk of our public money. Further, the blood of our children has been too often pledged and spilled to protect the rights of companies to dominate the world's markets, resources, and labor pools. Appeals to patriotism and propaganda fool us into believing that we operate in defense of democracy around the world. We do not.

We will never have the resources needed to protect ourselves against environmental harms unless we see clearly what type of nation we've become and change our destructive pattern. To continue preparing for war is to keep open a useless second front that we ought no longer to invest with a false security rationale. The damage we have done and are doing to ourselves is well beyond the capacity of any of our enemies, real or imagined.

No matter what your background may be, you are very likely to delight in solutions to our environmental crisis through use of the domestic violence clause. To borrow a word from my scientific friends, you are likely to find that solutions through the use of Article IV, Section 4 are "exquisite."

CHAPTER 2

CORNERSTONE OF THE CONSTITUTION

Make no mistake, your domestic violence clause was not an afterthought tucked into one of the back sections of the Constitution for a small purpose. It was the very cornerstone of the Constitution. The need to face up to problems addressed by Article IV, Section 4 caused the delegates from the thirteen states to exceed the authority given to them by their states. They had been sent to the convention in Philadelphia with orders limited to amending the Articles of Confederation. Instead, they scrapped the Articles, closed their meeting to public view, and created a different constitution with a new central government powerful enough to protect them in emergent situations.

Under the Articles of Confederation, the central government was a toothless tiger. It had no power to tax either the thirteen states or citizens directly, even for the money to pay Revolutionary War debts. As a result, soldiers who fought with General Washington had been given near worthless federal scrip. Many of these men were now farmers in the process of losing their lands because they could not pay their own debts.

An unusually high number of farm foreclosures in Massachusetts resulted in Shays' Rebellion. The impoverished and powerless federal government could only stand by and watch. The State of Massachusetts was barely able to maintain order against that insurrection. At one point, a thousand armed farmers marched against government troops at the Springfield Armory.[1] The lack of security was not limited to internal threats. There was a fear of invasion as well. The British, Spanish, French, and native Americans appeared poised to take all or parts of the existing states.

Against this backdrop of threats to the survival of our young country, delegates began arriving at the Constitutional Convention in

7

Philadelphia in May of 1787. Travel in those days was limited to horseback or carriage. Bad weather often made roads impassable. Those who arrived early for a first meeting on the morning of May 14 would wait eleven days until a majority of the thirteen states represented finally assembled on May 25. The eleven days were spent in active private discussions during which the leadership of America exchanged information and assessed the position of their young country.[2]

This experiment in self government was going badly. Shays' Rebellion had been put down and concluded only the year before. In the Rebellion, Europeans saw the seeds of self destruction in the new United States. We were, in their view, without power to keep internal disruptions from occurring. Worse, we were without power to deal effectively and quickly with internal disruptions after they began.

Could a nation long exist with a federal government that was little more than a powerless debating society? If there were another attack by a foreign power, would citizen soldiers, still unpaid from the Revolutionary War, enlist to repel an invader? To the delegates, these were not idle questions they wrestled with while awaiting a quorum. The delegates, many of whom were signers of the Declaration of Independence, had pledged their property, their reputations, and their very lives to the American experiment. Owing to an obvious lack of power in the federal government, the experiment was headed toward disaster.

The first speaker on the first day of business, May 29, was Edmund Randolph of Virginia. He reflected the fears of all the delegates by noting that the European governments were expecting the "downfall" of the United States. His first and most vehement point was the need to have a central government strong enough to assure survival in the face of threats both domestic and foreign, from rebellions and from invasions.[3] Clearly, what was to become Article IV, Section 4, the obligation on the part of the federal government to protect us against invasion and domestic violence, was the first and most significant order of business on the minds of the delegates to the Convention.

There was general agreement with Randolph's assessment of the need to create a strong central government. The gentlemen there assembled quickly moved beyond their instructions to merely amend the Articles of Confederation. As a result, they closed the meeting to public view,[4] scrapped the Articles, and began to construct a new central government—one that had as its main purpose the fulfillment of the obligations imposed by Article IV, Section 4, to protect us against both invasion and domestic violence.

CHAPTER 3

WHAT THEY MEANT BY DOMESTIC VIOLENCE

Compared to today, the environment in the United States of 1787 was pristine. George Washington had been selected to preside over the Constitutional Convention. The position required steady nerves and a calm disposition. Washington, throughout the summer of 1787, found the necessary rest and recreation by fishing the streams in and around Philadelphia and nearby Camden, New Jersey. Today, fish from those very streams, if there be any, are too tainted with pollutants to be safely eaten. If our world has become so grossly different from that of the framers, how can it be said that their use of the phrase, "domestic violence," was intended by them to fit our circumstances of pollution and environmental harm? The answer is that an analysis of their words, their conduct, and the context of both leads one to conclude, with little question, that the framers intended the domestic violence clause for our use in dealing with our environmental harms.

First, the framers understood well that it was a Constitution they were putting together, not a plan for the setting up of a particular local government. They used words that would fit changing circumstances, general words that would work in the future, not words likely to strangle meaning and progress. Edmund Randolph, himself, wrote about how a constitution was to be composed. Only simple and precise language was to be used. Only general propositions were to be stated. Otherwise, he said, government would be clogged by permanent, unalterable provisions that could not be shaped to fit the needs of later times and events.[1] Even a cursory review of the Constitution reflects that words were used in their general, commonly understood, sense. The absence of legal jargon is obvious.

Perhaps the largest motivation for the framers to use readily understood words was the fact that they did not take upon themselves final authority for adoption of the Constitution. The document was prepared to be ratified, after lengthy public discussions, in the States. The last word was to be that of the people. For that reason, plain language was mandatory.

What the framers thought of Shays' Rebellion offers direct evidence of what they believed to be the core meaning of the phrase "domestic violence." Randolph made immediate reference to the Rebellion on that first day of the Convention. A thousand armed farmers marching on a government armory in Springfield, Massachusetts had the potential of bringing about significant harm.

There were, however, two aspects to the actions of those farmers. After peaceful petitioning failed, they, in the fall of 1786 (five years after surrender of the British), by force of arms, prevented judges from convening courts in various parts of the State. They were directly challenging the right of the State of Massachusetts to have Court sessions that would result in farm foreclosures and sentences to debtors' prison.[2] Many of those men, as previously noted, had been soldiers in General Washington's army who still had not been paid for their services. Rebellion against lawful authority was, therefore, their intention. They were willing, if necessary, to use a show of force and threaten violence. The two aspects of their actions, therefore, were insurrection against authority and the potential of violence.

The important point is that the framers, early in the drafting process, used the term "violence" instead of "insurrection" in Article IV, Section 4, even though the showcase event, Shays' Rebellion, was far more an example of insurrection than violence. In fact, historians have recorded that the farmers advanced on the armory never believing that their brethren in military uniforms would fire upon them. To their shock and surprise, the soldiers began firing. The farmers fled without returning a single shot. The few resulting casualties occurred during a full and disorderly retreat.[3] The domestic violence clause in Article IV, Section 4 was intended, therefore, to have as its central focus, not just physical challenges to authority, but any activities having the potential to bring about significant harm. Prevention of significant harm is the core meaning of the protection we are owed by the U. S. government against "domestic violence."

Has the meaning of the term "violence" changed from when the framers used it to today? No. The word has had a consistency of meaning from the year 1290 to the present; it concerns the infliction of harm or injury upon persons or property.[4] Here is a sampling of usage from the Oxford English Dictionary that is significant to the time of the Convention:

- From Pennsylvania Colonial records of 1704: "If they were clear of violences done lately upon a family of the English."

- By Fletcher around 1619: "They have done violence unto her Tomb, Not granting rest unto her in the grave."

- By Hobbes in 1651: "Promises proceeding from fear of death or violence are no covenants."

- From a letter by Walpole to G. Montagu dated Dec. 23, 1759: "Has your brother told you of the violences in Ireland?"

- Samuel Johnson's *Rasselas*, published in 1759, included the phrase: "The violence of war admits of no distinction."

Interestingly, the term violence was often used to describe the effects of chemicals and poisons upon the body:

- From the world famous *Cyclopaedia*, compiled by Ephraim Chambers and published in 1758: "Sublimate, Corrosive Sublimate...is then a violent poison, which corrodes and destroys the Parts of the Body with much Violence."

- Chaucer, in *The Pardoner's Tale*, about 1386, described the strength of a poison as being capable of causing death in a shorter time than it takes to walk a mile: "This poyson is so strong and violent."

- A 1780 reference designated, "Newgate Cal. v. 232," is quoted as follows: "In the morning she perceived a violent smell of sulphur."

Man's capacity for inhumanity toward his fellow man was well known to the delegates. Few disagreed with Alexander Hamilton's assessment that "men were ambitious, vindictive, and rapacious." Domestic dangers were thought to be "more alarming than the arms and arts of foreign nations."[5] Near the very end of the Convention, on August 30, 1787, a motion was made to strike out "domestic violence" and insert in its place the term "insurrections." That motion was defeated.[6] They knew we were fully capable of self destructing and did not wish to limit Article IV, Section 4 to any one method then known.

From the crucial vote on that motion, from the generally accepted meaning of the term "violence," and from the context of discussions at the Convention, we can fairly assume that the framers meant the following when they used the phrase "domestic violence:" harm that we would do to ourselves and one another of such a nature as to be beyond the police powers of the states to contend with and be of such a magnitude as to threaten survival.

Is it accurate to say that the framers intended the domestic violence clause to be applicable to circumstances like our present environmental plight? Of course. The deepest core value expressed

14

in Article IV, Section 4 is protection to assure survival. Environmental threats are harms we've done to ourselves and to one another. They are well beyond the powers of the states to solve, and they threaten our survival.

If by some magic the framers could speak to us today, they would say that our 20th century was the very epitome of violence directed at ourselves and each other. Our power to do harm has far outstripped our wisdom. In the words of William Shakespeare, we truly did "write sorrow on the bosom of the earth."[7]

CHAPTER 4

IF YOU CAN KEEP IT

When the Constitutional Convention concluded and the secret was out that a new governmental system had been created, one citizen is alleged to have rushed up to Benjamin Franklin and asked, "What kind of government is it?" Franklin responded, "It's a republic, if you can keep it."[1]

As Franklin spoke, George Washington may yet again have been heading in the direction of a much needed favorite fishing spot, one of many in a yet unspoiled landscape. The Industrial Revolution, well begun in England, had not yet arrived in America. America was then a pre-industrial society.[2] Products like nails, shoes, spinning wheel irons, and cutlery were made here by hand by people who called themselves "mechanicks."[3] The steamboat would gain acceptance in 1807.[4] Oil would not be discovered in Titusville, Pennsylvania until August 29, 1859.[5] The American chemical industry began to be a significant participant in production and world trade as a result of World War I (1914-1918), often referred to as the "chemists' war."[6] The assembly line was first introduced by Henry Ford in 1913.[7] The full brunt of our heedless pollution and spoiling of America would not begin until World War II (1942-1945). The ensuing environmental destruction of the country was most aptly described by Ralph Nader in 1971 as "relentless environmental violence."[8]

It has been more than two hundred eventful years since Franklin's response. Time and the onslaughts of our relentless environmental domestic violence have changed both the focus and the magnitude of a question and answer that is more appropriate for our circumstances. We now find ourselves asking if our *world* is envi-

17

ronmentally safe. The answer is that the Earth is yet a viable home and will remain so, *if you can keep it.*

The most appropriate and generally accepted statement of the precariousness of our present position with regard to the environment came from the Worldwatch Institute in 1987:

> No generation has ever faced such a complex set of issues requiring immediate attention. Preceding generations have always been concerned about the future, but we are the first to be faced with decisions that will determine *whether the earth our children inherit will be inhabitable.*[9] (emphasis added)

Franklin is long gone, but his steady gaze remains. Whether we can maintain a viable Earth for our children is not a challenge exclusively for our presidents and our representatives. He would demand that we all take part in order to assure survival. Whether you and I are ready to accept responsibility is no longer important. Whether you and I feel capable of the job is beside the point. Circumstances have made it our task. The framers have given us a tool large enough to do the job–the domestic violence clause in the Constitution. "Pick it up," Franklin would urge. "You are fearfully close to making this planet uninhabitable for your children. We created the domestic violence clause just for this eventuality. You had best use it," he would say, "subordinating all lesser agendas and putting all the human and financial resources into the effort that you can. And you must persevere in that effort until the danger is passed. If this is not a time to use the clause, if this environmental plight of yours is not a condition of domestic violence, I am hard put to say what is. Don't tarry; pick it up."

CHAPTER 5

A CLAUSE FOR THE PEOPLE

How does one go about picking up the tool–the domestic violence clause–so that it can be used to get us out of environmental danger? Do we just hire a lawyer and start a lawsuit? No, not in this case. That clause, in order to work, is to be set in motion by the people. *You* are to do it directly. Let's open this time capsule and examine more closely the road map left for us by the framers. Article IV, Section 4 of the U. S. Constitution says:

> The United States shall guarantee to every state in this union a republican form of government, and shall protect each of them against invasion; and on application of the legislature, or of the executive (when the legislature cannot be convened) against domestic violence.

Don't be put off by the words "to every state in this union" and "each of them." In reading the Section, just substitute "you" for both of those phrases. The 1868 U. S. Supreme Court case of *Texas v. White*[1] clearly held that the word "state" in Section 4 refers to the people and not to the states as governmental entities. States are merely legal abstractions; people, on the other hand, are vulnerable, capable of suffering, and in need of protections. The guarantee of a republican form of government and the protections against invasion and domestic violence are personal IOUs from the United States directly to you and to your friends, families, and communities.

Our road map begins with the "on application" portion of Section 4. By setting forth that simple procedural starting place, the framers clarified where we must begin, what states must do, and what the federal government must do. Emergency conditions of domestic violence, just like invasions by foreign nations, require clear

19

lines of authority in order to ensure survival. To the federal government falls the burden of protection–the marshaling of all necessary human and financial resources to meet the threat. The state legislatures are to open public discussions as to whether a condition of domestic violence exists. Are the harms of such a nature as to threaten survival? Does the particular state possess sufficient resources and have adequate power to effectively deal with the crisis in the time required?

Such discussions are *political* in nature. They are not legal issues for lawyers to argue and for courts to decide. Courts do not generally make basic societal policy decisions. They defer, whenever possible, to legislatures and the executive branches. And when the Constitution is so clear that a domestic violence clause application for protection should come to the federal government from one or more state legislatures, you can be assured that courts will be little inclined to rule, themselves, on whether there exists a condition of domestic violence. Justice Frankfurter, in the 1946 U. S. Supreme Court decision of *Colegrove v. Green*,[2] set the tone in this regard for both the guarantee portion and the protection clauses of Section 4 when he said that "violation of the great guaranty of a republican form of government in States cannot be challenged in the courts." In other words, deciding on whether a condition of domestic violence exists is not for lawyers to argue about and for courts to decide. While there are some who believe that courts might agree to hear an Article IV "domestic violence" case,[3] at the present time, Frankfurter's words dominate the question. Such issues are for the people to decide in their state legislatures. And once made, those decisions are not likely to be challenged in the courts. The people will have spoken about a political decision.

There is another reason why courts are unlikely to decide that they should hear a case to determine whether a condition of domestic violence exists, and it has to do with financial resources. Since the first Earth Day in 1970, hundreds of environmental laws have been passed and implemented at the federal, state, and local levels. Most of these laws require private parties, at their own expense, to take actions that are designed to clean up the environment or limit releases of and exposures to toxins. In other words, the role of the various government agencies in enforcing these laws is to get the private sector to take on the economic burden envisioned by the laws. In large part, the federal and state governments are simply collection agencies and private businesses are unwilling payers. That point has to be made crystal clear because of confusion created by the federal government when it named the most visible federal environmental cleanup program, the "Superfund." Most Americans, because of the use of that name, have a false understanding that some huge pot of public money exists out of which all the cleanups of dangerous places are going to be funded. Nothing could be further from the truth. By way of simplified overview, the "Superfund" essentially pays the salaries and expenses of federal employees in the Environmental Protection Agency (EPA) while they attempt to collect money from the private sector with which cleanups can be accomplished. So, with all of the hundreds of laws on the books, there is, with minor exceptions, only one funding source–the private sector. In a word, cleanup of the country under existing laws is an effort that has been fully *privatized.*

If a condition of environmental domestic violence were found to exist, many of those laws that so delegate financial responsibility to the private sector would be deemed to be in conflict with the assessment of ultimate responsibility on the federal government under Article IV, Section 4. Judges for over twenty-five years have toiled to adjudicate cases under those laws that have privatized the financial cleanup responsibility. They will not take it upon themselves to embrace a different Constitutional understanding, one that places ultimate financial responsibility, instead, on the United States government, before the people act politically to create a new public funding source. Judges alone can not reorder the funding priorities of a nation, no matter how correct a legal theory presented to them may be.

So, you're stuck. Courts won't hear you, and lawyers are far too busy with a host of environmental laws–with which they are doing quite well, financially. The task, however, is likely to go far more easily than you may imagine. The proof that there currently exists a condition of domestic violence–environmental domestic violence–is overwhelming. Indeed, the majority of people are fast concluding that our environmental problems do, in fact, threaten our survival. Further, many people now understand that the present environmental laws are woefully inadequate to assure survival.

CHAPTER 6

A CONDITION OF DOMESTIC VIOLENCE

The crux of our present condition of environmental domestic violence under Article IV, Section 4 involves our failure to focus on who and what we are–in essence, our *frailty*. In 1970, at the beginning of our modern environmental movement, René Dubos, a microbiologist with Rockefeller University, attempted to warn us about our frailty. Our biological and mental nature, shaped by a million years of genetic experience, he said, were essentially unchangeable. We might tolerate, in the short run, environmental stresses for which we were not designed, but the price of that tolerance would be twofold. First, there would be increases in disease. Second, and far more menacing to Dubos, there would be "distortions of mental and emotional attributes." He predicted that unless we used our human genetic limitations as a standard, we would begin to see, near the turn of this 20th century, development of "a form of life that will retain little of true humanness."[1]

We came nowhere near using human genetic limitations as a standard for limiting harmful practices and exposures to toxins. Accordingly, as René Dubos predicted, there have been dramatic increases in diseases. For example, the National Cancer Institute's statistics showed that all types of cancer recorded from 1950 through 1985 had increased. Breast cancer cases for 1985 affected 130,000 women, of whom 40,000 were dying annually from the disease. Non-Hodgkin's lymphoma more than doubled in both incidence and mortality over the thirty-six year period. Malignant melanoma, a skin cancer type most often fatal, by 1985 more than tripled in incidence and doubled in mortality since 1950.[2]

Not only were cancer rates increasing, but cancer was striking people at younger ages. Dr. Darrel Rigel, a research physician at

New York University Medical Center, recalls that it was unusual to see persons under the age of forty with skin cancer. Now, he often sees people with that disease in their twenties.[3] Seeing children even of tender ages with cancer is not the rare event it used to be.[4]

Another example of a dramatic increase in disease is asthma, an immune system disorder that increased among U. S. children ages six to eleven from 4.8 percent to 7.6 percent between the periods 1971-1974 and 1976-1980. The disease increased 29 percent in this country between 1980 and 1987. Sufferers in 1987 numbered some 9.6 million Americans, and deaths from the disease went from 2,891 in 1980 to 4,360 in 1987. Young people were disproportionately affected between 1980 and 1987; the rate of increase for those under twenty years of age was 40 percent.[5]

Although increases in disease are compelling, the far more menacing aspect of our public health decline, as Dubos predicted, are the "distortions of mental and emotional attributes," leading us to experience "a form of life that will retain little of true humanness." The evidence for that aspect of environmental domestic violence is all around us, all the time.

Our children die by suicide at rates that are unprecedented for any civilization at any time in human history. The suicide rate among teenagers has tripled since 1950.[6] The number of psycho-paths and youthful murderers is increasing.[7] What used to be "crimes of the century" are almost every day fare in America. Dr. Marvin E. Wolfgang of the University of Pennsylvania conducted a massive study in which he found that young men born in 1958 were much more involved in violence compared to a similar group born in 1945. Dr. Wolfgang described this "escalation of violent criminal-ity" as "a fearful sign for the public."[8] The United States has be-come one of the most violent societies in the world.

There were 1,262 drive-by shootings in San Antonio, Texas in 1993, and 19 people died as a result. One homeowner in that city decided to spend thousands of dollars to make his home bullet-resistant. His observation of the people responsible for the violence captures the very essence of Dubos' prediction of a form of life that will retain little of true humanness. The unidentified homeowner said that he never expected to be frightened by some children, "but you look into those kids' eyes, there's no soul there."[9]

The National Assessment of Educational Progress, a federally supported organization that monitors academic performances of American school children, points to the fact that students at all levels are now more deficient than students used to be in higher order thinking skills, abstract reasoning, and problem solving.[10] These are the children who, as Dubos put it in 1970, "will have been exposed from birth throughout their formative years to conditions that will almost certainly elicit maladaptive responses in the long run–not only organic diseases but also, and perhaps most importantly, distortions of mental and emotional attributes."[11]

Pulitzer Prize winning historian, Barbara Tuchman, in a 1987 article entitled "A Nation in Decline,"[12] decried America's "deteriorating ethics, poor performance, poor thinking, and lawlessness," saying that "it does seem that the knowledge of a difference between right and wrong is absent from our society, as if it had floated away on a shadowy night after the last World War." The qualities she saw as being in short supply are honor, truthfulness, discipline, a love of justice, and perseverance. Are any of them attainable without significant higher order thinking skills and abstract reasoning? Each of those qualities requires a high level of conceptual thinking and the ability to postpone immediate gratification. Impairment of the intellectual processes that allow for higher order thinking skills reduces our capacity for honor, truthfulness, discipline, a love of justice, and perseverance. Impairment translates to both a lack of civility and a lack of general mental capacity and is an attack on the very possibility of maintaining an ordered civilization.

Employers recognize that a significant percentage of Americans in the labor force are now properly characterized as being unable to solve problems. For that reason alone, we will have difficulty competing in the global economy.[13] But the problem of an impaired work force is only a small part of the story. We are an *impaired citizenry* facing challenges including damage to the Earth's protective ozone layer, global warming and climate changes, overpopulation, depletion of soil and water resources, breaks in the food chain, and recent precipitous declines of indicator species that warn us we are perilously close to a crash of our natural support systems. This is the wrong time to accept having an impaired citizenry. As the Worldwatch Institute has pointed out, "we are the first generation ever to be faced with decisions which will determine whether the Earth our children inherit will be inhabitable."

Just when we must be more brilliant, more daring, and more courageous than any previous generation, we are hobbled by our lack of mental acuity. Impairment, if not faced up to and corrected, will rob us of the power to make and implement decisions that will ensure a habitable Earth for our children. Continued impairment will cause the harshest of sentences to be executed upon our children. As General George Washington penned in his last wartime circular, "...with our fate will the destiny of unborn millions be involved."[14]

And make no mistake, if we fail to recognize that a condition of domestic violence under Article IV, Section 4 of the Constitution exists, and if we fail to do something about it, our children and grandchildren will not simply and mercifully die. They will be swept up in the unnamable sufferings of a country and a world that lacks the qualities of humanness. They will be forced to make their way in an inept and a brute society such as the world has never seen. Bestiality coupled with a modern capacity to do harm is a frightful specter.

Many people have actually begun to hope that the world will end. (Belief that the world can end is an ancient concept.) They understand how insensitive we've been to the natural world that supports us. Fearing we will not change, they embrace the idea that a merciful end will soon come to this fallen Earth. Robert Frost used this fascination with the possibility of planetary death in his poem, "Fire and Ice." There, using a child-like meter, he posed the deadliest question; by which of two means, fire or ice, passion or indifference, is the world more likely to end? We, however, should take no solace in the thought that the world can end. It is by far more likely to survive as a hostile and an insufferable place, without an exit as easy as death.

My poem, "Taking Stock" is a dialogue following Frost's "Fire and Ice," from a vantage point of some forty years after his work:

TAKING STOCK

I do not picture

An end of life

In merciful stroke

Of fire or ice,

But a turning

From the human

Well begun.

Poisoned

Cell and soul

From leavings

Of false gods

In the Chemical Age

For which

We were not made.

No longer strapping

Nor dream filled,

Language already

Like chatter

In tree tops,

The great weapon

Truth

Unrecognizable.

Now having to stop

A turning well begun

Toward dark places.

Artists and writers are usually excellent forecasters of the ills of society and know well the direction we should take. Above all else, they train themselves, to *observe*. Societies can long practice group denial to the point of high folly;[15] most artists and writers cannot.

The theme of environmental assaults leading to an inept and a brute society is not new in the arts. Indeed, the relationship is a self-evident truth. Jack London's 1903 work, *The People of the Abyss*, described circumstances in East London, England. The writer observed that the city's air, filled with "sooty and tarry hydrocarbons" weakened its people both "mentally and physically." The children were "listless" and "without virility or stamina." Hardy newcomers from the farms took their places and were in turn "undermined" and "broken."[16] More recently, Joyce Carol Oates, in a short story entitled "Family," traced one family's descent into madness and brutality following a breakdown of society's environmental infrastructure.[17] Our society, at deep levels, well understands the direction in which we are headed. Popular movies carrying the theme of madness following societal breakdown include *A Clockwork Orange*, *Road Warrior*, *Mad Max*, and *Brazil*.

My poem, "Taking Stock," written in 1985, is yet another example of observation or vision that has the capability of being of service to society. Its message is exactly the same as that conveyed by René Dubos in 1970 when he warned that continuing exposures to toxic materials and conditions beyond the genetic experience of humans would lead to "a form of life that will retain little of true humanness." The message is proving itself to be correct.

Past societies paid respectful attention to the visions of people they learned to accept as truthful, predictive, and probable. Visions are not meant to be soothing. If beneficial, they are *accurate*. A desert tribe tries to avoid moving in the wrong direction at the wrong time by paying attention to its members with the imaginative vision to keep the group safe.

We are not unlike that desert tribe. We are beginning to notice that we have environmental problems threatening survival and diminishing human potential. Do we boldly organize around the Constitutional concept of the domestic violence clause? Do we reject it and continue with our present legal structure? Just like that tribe, we can go the wrong way and lose. Time is not on our side. We are the first generation ever to be faced with an abyss of such dreadful proportions.

Institutional scientific inquiry, as we have practiced it, in this matter is unavailing. In situations touching public health and the environment, Americans want very much to believe that the scientists are the "sole guardians of rationality."[18] The institutions, however, within which the vast majority of scientists work are unduly burdened with high research costs, a flawed patronage system,[19] and debilitating conflicts of interest.[20] Little can be expected from "official" science. By the time it allows for decisions on the existence of danger (if it ever does) and by the time it lays out a course of action (if it ever does), we are likely to be well beyond help. The type of scientist most likely to be useful in Article Four discussions will be, as Albert Einstein described the likes of Max Planck in 1918, a "solitary fellow" struggling to make for himself an "intelligible picture of the world," fully using his "intuition."[21] That practitioner will no doubt understand what authors William Broad and Nicholas Wade have said: "Science is not removed from the wellsprings of art or poetry, nor is it the only cultural expression of rationality."[22]

I strongly urge that we embrace the vision of Dubos. It has been shown, in adequate enough depth, to be correct. It has the feel of common sense and appropriateness. In present circumstances, it is the best warning we'll get. Dubos' prediction is observable in our streets, in our schools, and in our hearts; it is the epitome of a condition of domestic violence under Article IV, Section 4. If a brute world that is, in the words of Dubos, "marked by distortions of mental and emotional attributes," no longer resembling true humanness, is not a condition of domestic violence, what in God's name would be?

Dubos died in 1981, the year that I began to conceive of the possibility of declining human potential as a result of exposures to toxic materials. I neither heard of him nor read his works until after I wrote the first draft of the poem "And So Near" in 1985. Sometimes a towering spirit so imbued with love and concern for us, a *bodhisattva* (a being committed to our liberation), can guide our steps even beyond death. I feel compelled to report that the first draft of "And So Near" was written under unusual circumstances in *one* night in 1985.

I was then quite busy in the general practice of law. Days were hectic and cluttered and involved dealing with a maze of details growing out of a wide array of cases. The realization that toxins were affecting us all behaviorally was a thread that had been weaving in and out of my consciousness since 1981–a thread I sometimes picked up, sometimes denied as a possibility, and sometimes researched when time allowed.

Dusk had just begun as I was driving home that night through residential streets. I had not yet put on my headlights. Then about two hundred feet ahead, a tree some fifty feet in height suddenly became incandescently white. I slowed the car and parked. After a short interval, the brilliant white, shimmering light began softly and gently falling to the ground and disappearing. In a moment or two, the tree was again green and leafy.

I got out of the car and searched the area, expecting to find some apparatus that caused the white light–wires, bulbs, fireworks, etc. I found nothing of the sort. Later, and with some research, I discovered that similar events had occurred and were occurring with regularity to people throughout the world. There was nothing particularly special about me or any of the others who had seen such things. The purpose of the unusual events appears to be an effort by a higher power or a higher aspect of ourselves to get us to focus and give critical attention to some part of our lives and thoughts that we may have relegated to a back burner.

I seemed to know in an instant what I was to do that night. I rushed home and told my wife what had happened. I immediately thereafter started writing poetry, putting on paper the threads and snatches of environmental awareness that had begun to appear in my consciousness since 1981. The pen moved with a speed that leads me to believe that René Dubos may have wanted to issue one more warning. He and others like him could have been talking through any of us who showed some sensitivity. I ask you to consider "And So Near" to be René Dubos trying again, using what he had at hand, to speak to you, to warn you.

AND SO NEAR

GOD: You are not

As you were,

Beloveds,

When we began

And wonder

First quickened

So long a journey

Ago.

Though I am

Everywhere

For you,

You stumble

Eyeless

31

With but steps
Remaining.

No enemy
Leads you
In slavery
Through triumphal arch.
You maim your own,
Heedless
Forgetful
Of your frailty.

The garden
Earth,
Yours to tend
And keep,
That keeps you,
Is now alien
And brings you
Low.

Beloveds,
Into the winds
And the waters
Have you put
Metals

A CONDITION OF DOMESTIC VIOLENCE

You now
Eat and breathe.
They rob you
Of who you are.

Maker of elements,
You charted,
Mixed and matched,
Siring compounds
In the millions,
Of which
You know nothing.
Yet you flung them too
Into the winds
And the waters.

Now the compounds
And the metals
Are as much you
As bone and muscle.
They rob you
Of your will.
You are not
As you were.
I fear
Losing you.

I cry for you.

When reason
Is full fled,
You'll be unlike
My creatures
Solemn,
Pacific,
Graceful
On the Earth.
You will be
Plague
Unto one another
As days hold
No promise
Stronger
Than death.

The metals
And the compounds
Are as poisons
Lodging in every
Smallest particle
In every part
Of you
Are they.

And not you

Alone.

You've dug

And scraped,

Combined and spilled,

Till now

All my creatures

Are heavy laden

With them,

The metals

And the compounds.

Poisons smash

The fine filigree

That is

Your soul,

Meant to hear

Movements of heavens

And my whispers.

Heavens sing still.

I whisper.

Your soul,

Splintered

And confused

Is all
In discord,
Crying out
Wearily.

The precious flame
In you
Burns low
And less true,
Yet it is
The only flame
You know
And so believe
All is well.

So will you believe
That all is well
Even in the madness
To come,
Which you will
Also call
Civilization.

I hear you
As you
Cast about

A CONDITION OF DOMESTIC VIOLENCE

More metals

And compounds

Saying all the while

The risk of death

Is small,

Forgetting of madness,

Of illness,

Of grief

That can so crush

And make you yearn

For death.

While you speak,

The metals

And the compounds

Flow and rush

To the eyes

And every particle

Of every part

Of your babies,

Victims

Whose lives

Are dimmed,

Altered,

Diminished,

Without pity.

The tiniest

Of the smallest

Particles

In the unborn

Are tender

Spun webs

Upon which

Is written

In my hand

The way

Of that child

And the path

Of all men.

The strongest

Of you,

In your fiercest

Of pride

Are never more

Than those webs

And that writing,

Which is

As nothing

To the metals

And the compounds.

Mother and father
Bring to the nest
Foods of the garden
And waters
Now laden
With poisons
That stalk
In soft places.
The milk
Of her breast
Threatens.

The path
You choose
For the young
Is disease,
Misery,
Ignorance.

In time,
To them
The book
Will be
But marks on paper
Meaning nothing.

The parables
Will be
Puzzlement.

Sadness
Overcomes me.
So much promise
Is now
Ashes.

None of my creatures
Bring down
Their own
As do you.
Would that you killed
In rage,
I would understand.
Would that you killed
In war,
I understand that.
Would that you killed
In sport,
I would even
Understand then,
Having seen
So much.

But you kill

For your ease,

Your comfort,

Giving it the name

Progress.

That quest,

A fool's romp,

Has no end,

Short of losing

The wit

To know

When you've

Had enough.

By then,

The will

To stop

The killing

Is no more.

Most victims

Do not fall

In your view.

Believe me,

They do fall,

Weighted down

In every

Last particle

With the metals

And the compounds

Crushing thin strands

Within

That make up

Life.

I hold

In my hands

Creatures you have

Killed

And turned

From life.

I weep.

So few strands

Need you break

To hobble

A soul.

Already

Your discourse

Is that

Of the crazed.

Not distant

Is an end

Of truth.

A CONDITION OF DOMESTIC VIOLENCE

You
Who were meant
To be stewards
On the Earth
Leave metals
And compounds
In pools
Of elegant chain,
Deadly,
Taking victims
From now
Till longer
Than is all
The history
Of which you have
Record and recollection.

Hear me now
As never before.
You rush
To darkness,
Forgetting
As you have
That you must
Do more

Than believe in me.

You must nourish.

You must love.

You must understand.

Do I speak

That any

May hear?

What remains

Of will in you?

Study my tree

That stands

Quietly

Doing miracles,

Changing the nature

Of matter,

Not once

Dropping poison

At its feet.

If you can not

Do the same,

Do none of it.

Your time

In drunken delight

Of yourselves

Is over.

Feel the sweetness
Of the Earth.
Listen to its song.
Be as close to it
As a baby
Fed of it.
I am a wind
Blowing softly
Through you
And all things.
Touch me.

Listen not
To false gods
Of ease
And greed
Whose priests
Do harm
For coin.
Put aside war.
You have
No enemy
That rivals you
In destruction.

You must scour

In every corner.

Return to the Earth

What is best

Returned.

Heal wounds

Too small to see.

Purify all.

Can you

Put aside

Hatred?

Give up

Ease?

Curb greed?

Live with an ethic

Equal

To your power?

Look deeply enough

Within

To find love

That allows you

To choose

Life?

This is your work

Upon the Earth.

It will take

All that you are

And all that you have

To do it.

By this

And this

Alone

Shall you

Be judged.

MAN: I am afraid.

GOD: But you are

So near.

MAN: Show me

The way.

GOD: You know

The way.

Hurry.

CHAPTER 7

THE GOOD NEWS

You have just waded through sorrowful information about how both diseases and functional impairments are diminishing our lives and our potential. You envision the arrival of an inept, brute society that would lack capacity to solve the larger environmental problems which face this Earth. You may be haunted, as am I, by Barbara Tuchman's observation: "...it does seem that the knowledge of a difference between right and wrong is absent from our society, as if it had floated away on a shadowy night after the last World War." Is that not, as Dubos predicted, the onset of "a form of life that will retain little of true humanness"?

So where is the good news? The good news is threefold: First, we have an accurate diagnosis of our most fundamental problem. Second, knowing the diagnosis, we can proceed to a cure. Third, the domestic violence clause is available to us so that we can marshal resources necessary to bring about the cure.

The malady of aberrant behavior which has come to dominate our society has been brought about largely by conditions and exposures to toxins in amounts that are wildly beyond our genetic experience. The source of the problem thus recognized, it is within our grasp to solve. We are not (as many have become fond of saying) evil; we are ill and can choose to become well.

We are suffering more from *morbidity* (a disease state) than from a lack of morality. Writing about lead, author Donald F. Carr pointed out the probable way in which that metal causes brain dysfunction:

49

> There can be no doubt that the exposure of Americans to industrial lead is several orders of magnitude greater than God designed humans to bear... Lead can break through the blood-brain barrier. In the brain the lead may interfere with the synthesis or breakdown of neurotransmitters...I am worried about something more subtle and far-reaching than cancer. I am worried about lead contamination as a chemical factor in the undesirable lowering of intelligence and productivity–in general the drop in psychic energy of the American people as a whole... Lead poisoning–chronic plumbism–may be responsible for the decline and fall of the United States of America.[1]

Dr. Herbert L. Needleman, in a 1996 article published in the *Journal of the American Medical Association*, described a study that confirmed Donald Carr's fears. That study involved over 800 Pittsburgh schoolboys. Dr. Needleman found that the more lead they had in their bones, the more likely it was that they would engage in aggressive acts and delinquent behavior. He aptly characterized lead as a "brain poison that intereferes with the ability to restrain impulses."[2]

The good news is that there are easy ways to test every child and every adult in the country for the presence of lead. We know how to get lead out of our bodies and should begin doing it on a massive scale tomorrow. An effective mobilization to do those things, as well as to reduce further exposures, can be organized and funded under the domestic violence clause. That's what the clause was designed to do. To attain that level of protection from a harm we have done to ourselves and each other is the principal reason we created the federal government in the first place. The Constitutional obligation of protection under Article IV has been triggered by the existence of the lead in us that, according to Carr and others, threatens to bring about our destruction.

Societal decline from chronic lead exposure is nothing new. Drs. Needleman and Sergio Piomelli, leading researchers on the effects of low level lead exposure, note that the "increase in psychiatric disturbance in upper class Romans may have been related to lead exposure from plumbing and wine additives and thus was in part responsible for the decline of Rome."[3] The significant difference between ancient Rome and modern America is that our lead exposures cross class lines and are more evenly distributed in our population. Dr. Jonathan E. Ericson, an anthropologist, compared the bones and teeth of Peruvians buried 1600 years ago with those of 20th century Americans. The amount of lead in the bones and teeth of the average modern man proved to be 500 times greater than lead in the Peruvians studied.[4]

The madness of Emperors Caligula and Nero may well have resulted from preventable lead exposures. We can no more condemn them for their excesses than we can condemn our own people for bizarre, antisocial, or even criminal behavior stemming from such exposures. We have victimized ourselves and are suffering morbidity from exposure to a host of modern chemical agents. Jerome O. Nriagu, of the National Water Research Institute in Ontario, Canada, worries that the results of our exposures will continue to be misconstrued: "If it isn't lead," he says, "it could be PCB's, dioxin, or whatever. They'll think we were crazy."[5]

While we have busied ourselves with condemnation and recrimination, Lewis Regenstein, author of *America the Poisoned*, observed the root causes of our deterioration. It was coming about unnoticed, difficult to measure, and easy to discount:

> Toxic substances in the environment may be affecting how we think, feel, and act to a degree that may be impossible to fully assess. In addition to physical illness, toxic chemicals and metals such as lead, mercury, and cadmium appear to be causing mental, emotional, and behavioral problems among a large segment of the population. Chemicals, food additives, and drugs are not generally tested for such effects; but since subtle behavioral changes are often difficult to detect, they may be extremely widespread throughout the population.[6]

The road to wellness begins by facing the fact that the societal declines we see all around us have, in large part, a physical basis. Those declines result from a myriad of interacting vectors of environmental harms that are, at the same time, direct, indirect, multiple, and beyond being readily measurable. The problem is of such magnitude and complexity that the only entity, public or private, that can conceivably respond appropriately to this public health challenge is the federal government. The only governmental mechanism by which the task can be accomplished is the domestic violence clause in Article IV, Section 4 of the U. S. Constitution.

In times of crisis, the government that bears responsibility must act quickly and decisively. It has always been so. When Joseph interpreted the Pharaoh's dreams to mean that Egypt would face death by famines, the Pharaoh quickly built granaries and reordered that nation's priorities to assure survival.[7] Benno Jacob, a commentator on the Bible, observed that Joseph interpreted to Pharaoh not his dreams but his duties.[8]

That story is critically germane with one insight added. We must be both Joseph and the Pharaoh. In our form of democracy, crises require citizens to rouse themselves and each other. Citizens have to actively shape the government they need for the challenges they face.

The good news is that we have found the road to take, yet in time to make a difference. We know the way, but we must hurry.

CHAPTER 8

PUTTING RESOURCES INTO EDUCATION

In the early 1980s, I spoke to a physician who did public health work for a state government. Cadmium and lead, even at very low doses, diminish children's learning capacity.[1] At that time, however, the connection between exposures and learning was little studied. I asked the physician about testing children at two apparently identical schools, one of which, being close to a highway, was near a source of airborne cadmium from automobile tires. He laughed and said he wouldn't come anywhere near such a project. It was, as he termed it, "far too political."

That conversation stays with me. At bottom, the man was saying that politicians were not about to spend money on moving either the school or the road just for the health of children. That being so, why should he risk his career by being a messenger carrying bad news to them?

Few people doubt that the intellectual capacity of our children has been and continues to be harmed by a host of toxins in the schools and in the environment. Neither public health officials nor teachers, however, can imagine society responding and putting adequate resources into actually solving the problem. Teachers with whom I've spoken have become sadly resigned to seeing students in the 12th grade struggle to understand concepts that were grasped easily by 8th graders twenty to thirty years ago. If you are a teacher or a parent, the way back to educational excellence is through your participation in bringing the domestic violence clause forward for public discussion. If hope is lost, all is lost.

You can begin to understand the power of the domestic violence clause by looking at its twin, the "invasion" part of Article IV, Section 4. The obligation to protect us is twofold; the United States must protect us from both "invasion" and from "domestic violence." If we were invaded, would any expense be too high a price to pay for the rapid deployment of a defense? If we were invaded, what competing public expenditures would have a higher priority than protection of the children from harm expected in that invasion? During the mobilization for World War II, nothing was allowed to take precedence over the war effort. We readily accepted personal privations and postponements. Winning the war came first. Winning the war of survival as a result of the present condition of domestic violence that we've created should entail no less an effort. We have harmed ourselves and the children for whom we are responsible more grievously than any enemy, just as the framers sensed we would.

Domestic dangers should not be considered secondary to foreign dangers. That is not how they were viewed by the framers. Alexander Hamilton's opinion on this point reflected the general consensus at the convention. Domestic threats were considered even "more alarming than the arms and arts of foreign nations."[2] And spending for whichever danger was at hand, in the words of the framers, "ought to know no other bounds than the exigencies of the nation and the resources of the community."[3]

The present exigency or danger is environmental domestic violence. It affects education most directly. The resources of the entire country can be made available immediately so that children need not be burdened with morbidity but can reach their full potential. Demanding necessary resources pursuant to the domestic violence clause is both a viable and a realistic course of action.

Students began sustaining physical damage that would affect their ability to learn long before they were born. Human development differs markedly from so-called lower forms of life in that a single egg is produced instead of millions. The reason this single-egg-at-a-time production has long sufficed for humans is that for nearly all of our genetic history, initial development was well protected within the human body.

Since America's great proliferation of chemical substances began in the 1940s, the developing embryo became an unappreciated *target* for toxins. Science placed itself into the service of industry, and little thought was given to harm that was occurring *in utero*. By the 1970s, the field of behavioral teratology "gained considerable momentum," owing to "the high proportion of children suffering from such developmental disorders as mental retardation, learning disabilities, and hyperactivity." It was believed by researchers at the time that "low doses of teratogens [toxins] cause behavioral deficits...by interfering with neuronal migration, dendritic differentiation, synaptogenesis, or myelinization."[4]

Taking neuronal migration as an example, an impaired student may have difficulty remembering instructions in a series or may be dyslexic. All of the neurons in that child's brain had to migrate from the place of creation to the optimum place of specialized use. Any one of a number of toxins could have interfered with the required migration. To use a borrowed term, the "hard wiring" of that child's brain is now something other than what it should have been. Teaching becomes as much a matter of creating *new* neural pathways as informing by way of reason and repetition.

Our error was and continues to be allowing chemical intrusions into a human embryonic world of exquisite sensitivity. The tolerances for error in this world are beyond our crude ability to imagine and to measure. We confused what little we knew of these mysteries with a false certitude that we were doing no harm. We were wrong. René Dubos' demand for a "human centered science" went unheeded.[5]

The resulting damage to children is both insidious and ongoing. The percentage of newborn children with some physical, mental, or learning defect had doubled from the late 1950s to 1981, going from 2 percent to 4 percent.[6] Even as school populations declined, the percentage of students classified as perceptually and neurologically impaired increased. In New Jersey, for example, in 1983-1984, the percentage so classified reached 14 percent.[7]

Scores on college entrance exams and elementary school standard tests declined dramatically in the 1960s and 1970s. According to a 1987 report by the Congressional Budget Office entitled *Educational Achievement: Explanations and Implications of Recent Trends*, changes in educational policy, quality of the schools, the number of minority students, television viewing, student use of alcohol and drugs, and the growing percentage of single parent households played at most "a modest role" in the declines.[8] The scores continue to remain low, even though the tests our children are taking have been made "drastically more simple" than those given in the 1970s."[9]

It may be true that we can improve our schools and our teachers. Certainly, it would be beneficial if we could keep students away from drugs, alcohol, too much television, and strife in the home. But, we could do all of that and still end up with an impaired student population, burdened by toxins well beyond their genetic heritage. The decline in educational achievement began, as Dubos predicted, in the 1960s, when the children were exposed from before birth and throughout their formative years to conditions that robbed them of their full innate potential for intellectual and emotional development. Is that not a condition of domestic violence that would mandate the use of every conceivable resource we can possibly muster?

It should come as good news that we can begin to turn around student performance toward excellence tomorrow. Once we come to recognize the true nature of our problem as not being exclusively an educational one but a public health matter, the road home can become a wide vista, well lit and filled with people working together with sufficient resources to do the job. With your help, attention to the domestic violence clause can bring that about.

CHAPTER 9

IMPROVING IN THE WORKPLACE

The fact that we can function as well as we do in the workplace is a tribute to the indomitability of the human spirit. A truly complete medical history of the work force should reveal that exposures to lead and other toxic substances began *in utero*. They were carried across the placenta.[1] PCBs (polychlorinated biphenyls–oil additives that allow machines to run at higher temperatures) might have been in the fish that mother ate with regularity. That chemical tended to impair neurological and intellectual development.[2] As a result of these and thousands of similar assaults, workers, from professionals to stevedores, were robbed, even before birth, of their full potential.

That complete medical history of the work force will include the fact that our food came largely from synthetic soil made from chemical fertilizers, insecticides, and herbicides. A host of other artificial food additives and sweeteners were our daily fare. The federal government does not test these items for their biochemical and behavioral effects.[3] The medical report should state as well, that our meat contained as many as 500 to 600 toxic chemicals. These chemicals went largely unmonitored by the U. S. Department of Agriculture,[4] and they were never tested for their capacity to do behavioral harm and diminish human potential.

If you were born after 1946, you probably reached puberty far earlier than your human genetic history could tolerate. Beginning in 1947, producers pumped growth hormones into our cattle, pigs, lamb, and poultry in order to bring meat, milk, chicken, and eggs cheaply to market in half the usual time. Growth hormone residues were taken into our bodies when we ate those foods. As a result, we tended to experience premature sexuality. One doesn't just skip over important pre-puberty stages without consequences. That loss has brought about significant emotional and intellectual impairment. Vast numbers of us in the work force, employers and employees alike and both non-professionals and professionals, now experience a resulting diminished capacity for formal operational thinking and a tendency toward attentional deficiency.[5]

The workplace is also rife with damaging, addictive behavior involving alcohol, drugs, gambling, and other negative conduct that people have difficulty shedding. Dr. Jack Nation, at Texas A & M University, believes there is a connection between such addictions and toxins. Rats routinely reject alcohol. Dr. Nation discovered, however, that when stressed by exposure to either cadmium or lead, they drink alcohol, apparently to be relieved of that stress.[6] In the same way, we are all being led toward damaging, addictive behavior. Exposure to toxins in amounts beyond our genetic experience is ongoing, and that exposure is fueling drug and alcohol abuse.

If you are an employer, chances are great that a significant percentage of your employees are functionally illiterate, meaning that they can read but cannot do complex tasks with the language. Janice Simpson, writing for the *Wall Street Journal*, described the 1987 report of the National Assessment of Educational Progress entitled *Literacy: Profiles of America's Young Adults* as "dismal" news for employers. In a test given to 3600 people between 21 and 25 years of age, "just over a third could calculate the cost of a restaurant meal with tip, and only 20 percent could interpret a bus schedule correctly. Across the board, researchers found, performance plummeted when the assigned tasks moved beyond the simpler levels."[7] From birth throughout the formative years, as René Dubos predicted, your employee was subjected to toxins beyond human genetic experience. Those exposures were the most significant factor in the lowering of your employee's functional capacity, his or her ability to be a fully able employee.

In this regard, Canada's experience with functional illiteracy is most informative. Canada receives enormous amounts of pollutants through the air and from places as far away as Louisiana, Texas, and Mexico.[8] Monte Hummel, president of the World Wildlife Fund Canada, calls this barrage of air pollution an attack on life at the microscopic level.[9]   As a result, the functional illiteracy rate among all Canadians is 24 percent. If test scores were just a trifle less charitably calculated, the rate of functional illiteracy among all Canadians would be 37 percent.[10]

A comparison of American and Canadian youth, ages 21 to 25, shattered all illusions about Canadian educational superiority. Both groups experienced difficulty in processing complicated information, and the Canadians fell down in that area just a bit farther.[11]

Canadians living around the Great Lakes have about 20 percent higher concentrations of toxic substances in their bodies than people living in other regions of Canada.[12]   Great Lakes expert, Henry A. Regier, reported that these children, when further exposed (through the food chain) to lake contaminants during gestation or nursing had greater tendencies for smaller birth weights and experienced more infectious illnesses. Such children, according to Regier, tend not to be "as sharp when they are contaminated."[13] Douglas J. Hallett, a former top Canadian government scientist, said that the effect of toxins is to "cause us to function so poorly that we're debilitated, not dead, but debilitated. And the prime target is children, because they're exposed to these things during their formative years."[14]

I have described the Canadian experience with functional illiteracy in order to show that we have been unfairly placing blame for that problem here at home. We have blamed the employee, his school, his union, his family life, and his society. Perhaps all of those institutions can be improved, but after improving them, your employee will still have trouble functioning.

Canadian society has, for many generations, been relatively stable. It was not war torn, as was ours. It was not race torn, as was ours. Urban and rural areas have maintained a certain consistency of life and style far beyond what we have managed to do. Family life has generally been less disruptive than ours. Labor-management relations have long been marked by accord. Immigration policies have been orderly and within limits. Finally, Canadian schools have been far more well run and adequately funded.

If *Canada* is experiencing a functional illiteracy problem even worse than ours, should we not be facing the fact that the probable effective cause of that deficiency is exposure to toxins beyond the human genetic capacity? No better experiment could have been devised to prove that our own problem of functional illiteracy is just another result of the existence in the United States of a condition of *environmental domestic violence*.

Under Article IV, Section 4 of the Constitution, federally funded efforts at testing and ridding the work force and their families of toxins can begin immediately. Sources of toxins, whether in our food, in the air, ground, or water can be shut off and cleaned up. Once chemical related morbidity is reduced, we can attain excellence in our places of work and live up to our full human potential.

Louis V. Gerstner, Jr., chairman of IBM, recently noted that "according to a survey by the National Association of Manufacturers, 30 percent of companies cannot reorganize work activities because employees can't learn new jobs, and 25 percent can't upgrade their products because their employees can't learn the necessary skills."[15] This condition need not persist; it can be directly and swiftly addressed by your attention to the domestic violence clause.

Barbara Tuchman's vision of spiritual impairment of our society serves this discussion well: "It does seem," she said, "that the knowledge of a difference between right and wrong is absent from our society, as if it had floated away on a shadowy night after the last World War." Nothing better expresses how sorely America has been beset by antisocial behavior in our various workplaces. From the professions has come far too much incivility and self seeking. From the markets has come a plethora of unethical behavior and short term profit taking at the expense of society. The knowledge of and a caring about the difference between right and wrong is a goal that can be attained. We are not an evil and a fallen people. When our present, insidious condition of toxic-driven environmental domestic violence is fully addressed, morbidity can and will be replaced by a higher spirituality in all that we are and all that we do.

CHAPTER 10

GETTING TO BE SAFE AT HOME

The last place that one expects to be at risk from harms that constitute environmental domestic violence under Article IV, Section 4 is in the *home*. Traditionally, the home was considered our castle, safe from the intrusions of both highwaymen and the sheriff. Until very recently, what we used and ate at home was well known to us and usually produced nearby. Being home was a reprieve from having to be on guard from dangers "out there in the world."

So, when we discover that our homes are unsafe, we, quite rightly, feel a betrayal of trust. The United States Environmental Protection Agency (EPA) has identified 1,000 indoor pollutants, of which at least 60 are carcinogenic. According to Lana Walker, an environmental scientist for EPA, "there is generally three times as much risk from breathing indoor air as outdoor air. Tens of thousands of cancer deaths alone are caused by indoor pollution every year." In addition to cancer, and more ominous, Walker relates that people are seriously and behaviorally affected by indoor air pollution and seldom know that it is the cause of their headaches, nausea, dizziness, drowsiness, respiratory ailments, persistent coughs, rashes, insomnia, lethargy, loss of memory, heart problems, and irritation to the eyes, nose, and throat.[1]

How has the home gone from being a safe haven castle to a place of risk? There are three major factors in the answer to that question. The first involves the focus of the American business community. In all of our history, we were never a significant trading country, sending finished goods to other nations for sale. Instead, we zeroed in on the "home market."[2] The chief target of that market has been the household, using sophisticated methods of advertising to increase sales through creating a desire for products. The second

61

factor was our euphoric embrace of science and the chemical industry. A. Cressy Morrison, in his well circulated 1937 book, *Man in a Chemical World*, expressed the understanding of the vast majority of Americans. "Our country would become a backward nation" without the chemical industry, "out of which grows civilization itself." Further, said Morrison, "the key to more abundant living lies not in political or economic hocus pocus, but in hard work undertaken and carried on in the light of scientific research."[3] The new gods of our age were chemistry and science. If science could make an item, we were honored to use it. Little, if any, thought was given to potential harm. We were ushering in a new age of splendor, plenty, and leisure. Producers of the newly discovered atomic energy, for example, promised that our use of it would be safe and unlimited; electric power from nuclear plants was to be "too cheap to meter."[4] We believed that also.

Thirdly, the government that was to protect us against harms that might be visited upon us by industry became essentially captured by industry. For a host of reasons, government agencies that were set up to look out for the welfare of the people, instead focused on benefiting industries that they regulated even though harm often came to the people as a result.[5]

One example should suffice to make the point clearly. As previously noted, beginning in 1947, farmers were allowed to give growth hormones to animals in order to bring meat and dairy products cheaply to market in half the usual time. Because science and chemistry had such an exalted position in society and because government was unduly solicitous of certain agricultural interests, the home market, you and I, were inundated with growth hormones, getting small amounts at practically every meal.

The results of our continuing ingestion of growth hormones include, as previously said, impaired intellectual functioning of children and premature sexuality. Regarding the latter, in the last fifty years, the age at which our children reached puberty has plummeted dramatically. We're beginning to see menstruation occur at eight years of age and pregnancy at nine. Hostile rape of females by boys under ten years of age has risen to epidemic levels today.[6] Forcible rapes by boys as young as seven are now a part of our puzzled juvenile justice system.[7] The national tragedy of teen pregnancy and the great number of resulting abortions are, in large part, the outcome of preteen sexuality caused by the careless use of hormones to augment meat and dairy production.

Society has been encouraged to blame the victims and their parents. "They," it is so often said, do not have "family values." Politicians using such a slogan will often attain public office and proceed to make matters worse by failing to focus on the real cause of the problem; government continues to be protective of an industry that continues to place even more growth hormones into our food supply and thus into our children. The most recent addition to this permitted use of growth hormones has been for the purpose of increasing the milk supply, even though we have long produced a surplus of milk. Worse, the federal government actually threatens sanctions against those milk producers who choose not to use the hormones and wish to tell their customers that their milk is free of them.[8]

Our children were not designed to have and contain sexual appetites at age seven. Being so early and abnormally stimulated has to affect their growth and development for the rest of their lives. In the language of René Dubos, these growth hormones are yet another toxic exposure that is wildly beyond human genetic history. As a result, our children are suffering "distortions of mental and emotional attributes." It is now commonplace in our society, lamented Gil Garcetti, the Los Angeles District Attorney, that youngsters, as never before, commit the most horrendous crimes imaginable without a second thought. And the increases in such violent crimes by children cross racial, class, and geographical boundaries.[9]

To make matters worse, when government allowed the meat and dairy industries to use growth hormones, yet another vector of harm to the population was created. Forced growth of the animals tended to weaken their immune systems. Accordingly, antibiotics had to be given to those animals and became a staple part of their diet. We have all been sorely affected by that indiscriminate use of antibiotics. Overuse of antibiotics given to farm animals has contributed to the mutation of strains of bacteria that are making effective medical intervention in human diseases more and more difficult. Dr. Alexander Tomasz of Rockefeller University, an authority on resistant bacteria, sounded an alarm at a recent meeting of the American Association for the Advancement of Science, saying that the problem of resistant bacteria could result in "nothing short of a medical disaster." He is of the opinion that the common bacteria, such as *Pneumococcus* and *Staphylococcus*, which are found around the world and in every home, may soon be resistant to antibiotics. Pneumonia then will become a killer disease,[10] right in the sanctity of our homes.

At present, a new strain of the common *E. coli* bacteria produces a toxin that has taken the lives of children in a matter of days. Robert B. Gaulin described his five year old son Eric's fight for life after attending a birthday party where tainted meat might have carried the bacteria. "What you're seeing," he said, "is your child essentially shutting down. All vital signs fall off a cliff, the red blood cell count goes way down, the white cells are up, and what you live for is the slowing down of that process."[11] Environmental domestic violence now touches the inner reaches of the sanctity of the home and turns even the most gentle activity into an ominous threat.

Now, as never before, a scraped knee brings fear of necrotizing fasciitis, skin destroying infections that are reported to be on the rise.[12] Those infections are more likely to take a bad course when a person's immune system has been weakened.[13] In the United States, the number of people with suppressed immune systems is growing.[14] As René Dubos warned, we were not designed for the thousands of toxins and combinations of toxins that we've made a part of our everyday experience. Exposure to powerful chemicals like dioxin, which suppresses the immune system, begins in the uterus and impairs fetal development.[15] While thus impaired, Americans experienced an unusual growth spurt in the last fifty years. That was brought about in significant part by our ingestion of the growth hormones that government allowed industry to put into our meat and dairy products. Just as the hormones weakened, by forced growth, immune systems of the animals, so have they weakened our own immune systems, setting us up for infections which will be all the harder to ward off.

The pattern of industry focusing on the home market, using a questionable chemical technology, and government allowing harm to be done to the people has become accepted conduct. Nowhere is this more clear than in our use of pesticides. Rachel Carson, in her book *Silent Spring*, in 1962, warned that the use of pesticides was dangerous and would not, in the end, control insects. She made an overwhelming case for the use of natural methods of pest control, with which we had long and successful experiences.[16] Notwithstanding her cogent warnings, pesticide use in the United States more than doubled since the 1960s.[17] As she predicted, insects have developed immunities and thrive. Crop loss to insects and weed pests was 32 percent in 1955. Despite the continuous, massive use of chemicals, crop losses actually increased to 37 percent in 1984.[18] Now, on a typical mass production farm, the soil has been spoiled and degraded to being simply the medium that holds the stalks up while chemical fertilizers and pesticides bring a tainted crop to market. These pesticides, which do not readily wash off our fruits and vegetables,[19] now find their way into our homes every day, as do the meat and dairy growth hormones. And, at bottom, most synthetic organic insecticides are nerve poisons that inhibit and interrupt human functioning at the cellular level. They can affect our reproductive cells, causing birth defects, infertility, and a myriad of illnesses resulting from genetic damage. We do not die immediately from such exposures, but these toxins become part of a complex web of factors limiting our human potential and making us ill, remaining all the while subtle and often unsuspected.[20]

Most troubling is the manner by which the government has made itself reluctant to stop the cycle of pesticide use. By law, in order for the United States to ban a pesticide, it must buy up and dispose of all unused stocks of that product at the taxpayers' expense.[21]

If the purpose of government is protection of the people, then we have strayed considerably from that path. The parade of dangerous products into the home market is allowed to continue. Quite simply, there has been control of government by economic interests (factions) seeking gain at the expense of the people. James Madison warned of the "violence of faction" as a "dangerous vice" by which particular interest groups motivated by gain would seek advantage even though such might be "adverse to the rights of other citizens or to the permanent and aggregate interests of the community."[22] In that way could a "stronger faction...unite and oppose the weaker."[23] The bulwark set up by the framers against the evil of faction was to be the elected representative "whose wisdom may best discern the true interest of their country and whose patriotism and love of justice will be least likely to sacrifice it to temporary or partial considerations."[24]

It hasn't worked out that way. In the 20th century, government has tended to treat the dominant economic interests as favored "clients" to the detriment of the people.[25] As a result, we continue to harm ourselves by a steady flow of toxins even into the sanctity of our own homes. Your children and mine, as a result, are experiencing a diminution of human potential that began *in utero*. Adults are no less affected. Much of the physical and emotional abuse that takes place in the home is attributable to behavioral declines brought about by toxins within us that are beyond our genetic potential to manage. Even the once innocent events around any home, like birthday parties and scraped knees, are now causes for fear. Owing to a decline in the Earth's protective ozone layer, a short time spent in the sunshine must now be considered potentially dangerous activity.

There is danger in believing that these circumstances were always so. Humans are far too adaptable for our own good. Our present condition is *new*. These times are beyond previous human experience. There presently exists a condition of environmental domestic violence so severe that it threatens the viability of our species and the viability of the support systems of our planet.

I have been involved in writing, researching, and talking to people about the environment since 1983. Every passing year has brought greater awareness to us all concerning the extent of our environmental problems. If I can generalize, by this time the vast majority of us are beginning to understand the depth of our problem. We, however, despair about the possibility of seeing it resolved. We would work and sacrifice–do anything–to protect our loved ones. We, however, are powerless to act together effectively until our government stops treating the dominant economic interests as its clients and begins to help us mobilize our efforts and our creativity. The anomaly is that we are headed toward a brute society on an uninhabitable planet with an impaired citizenry, and our central government has not even begun to consider a way to mobilize our courage, our strength, and our resources to meet the challenge.

Senator Charles Sumner, in 1867, described the guarantee portion of Article IV, Section 4, as the "sleeping giant in the Constitution."[26] He had urged President Lincoln to exercise complete control over the southern states using the theory that if they embraced slavery they could not provide the required republican form of government as guaranteed by Article IV. If the guarantee portion is a sleeping giant, the domestic violence clause is a *colossus*. The former simply requires a particular model of government by the states; the latter mandates effective federal protection during emergency conditions. That is the colossus the framers would have us harness to get ourselves to safety on our planet and in our homes.

Use of the domestic violence clause has the potential to mobilize all of us in the monumental work that must be done. Nothing short of total dedication of all our resources and all our people can get us back to safety. The genius of Article IV, Section 4 lies in the placement of absolute responsibility to focus unified, central government attention upon an emergency, subordinating all competing rights, interests, and agendas, gathering and expending the necessary human and financial resources, and maintaining that effort until the threat is abated.

For all that to happen, you, your neighbors, friends, and coworkers must begin to talk about and formulate the mission of the central government under the domestic violence clause. In turn, the federal government, with your full and personal participation, can direct the great undertakings that will be necessary to ensure our safety and our survival. Article IV, Section 4 is the road map in a time capsule left for us by the founders who knew that, in the end, we would be our own worst enemy.

The last time this country was totally mobilized for a public effort was World War II. Those who lived through that period and served either in the military or on the civil side are likely to be carrying, with pride, memories of answering a call to service. The founders would have us duplicate that effort. The present threat to our homes and families is no less ominous and far more immediate. The condition of environmental domestic violence that we have brought upon ourselves has already caused untold harm to Americans for over two generations.

CHAPTER 11

A SELF EXAMINATION

A project the size and scope of initiating emergency measures under the domestic violence clause ought to begin with some soul searching self analysis. The domestic violence clause is a people's clause to be implemented by us. If done thoughtlessly, the effort could further concentrate power in the hands of the few with disastrous results. Are we capable of doing the job and getting it right? What might be the most essential, personal ingredient we must possess in order to ensure success? I believe that the most necessary personal ingredient is a very simple thing–the ability *to be still* within ourselves.

We are, above all else, a highly distracted people. Between radio, television, VCRs, tape, and CDs, we have almost no time for silence, for reflection. Never before have people been able to experience such instant gratification of entertainment desires. In other times, to hear music required the gathering of musicians, travel, planning, and long anticipation. The event, experienced between stretches of quiet thoughtfulness, was likely to trigger imagination and leave enduring strands of memory. Now, we merely flick a switch to be bathed in favorite entertainments, along with the constant drone of advertising, managed news, and political posturing; we don't know *silence*.

We even define ourselves by our entertainments and our distractions without realizing how far they take us from knowing who we are. We sometimes catch a glimpse of that distancing mechanism just after a Superbowl game or at the end of a long awaited concert. But then another sport or attraction begins to take center stage. Another talk show host captures our focus.

Like Dr. Nation's alcohol drinking rats, do we cling so tenaciously to our distractions as a palliative for the stresses caused by toxins in us beyond our genetic experience? I'm certain to a large extent that's true. Whatever the reason, as a people, our ability to critically focus on events over time is extremely limited. Our civic awareness is a mile wide and an inch deep. We, the people, tend not even to know our own history; we are largely ignorant about world events; current political matters are summarily decided for us by wealthy and powerful interests. William Greider's book, *Who Will Tell the People*, is an excellent portrayal of just how those interests in America have profited and the vast majority of people have suffered in areas such as taxes, jobs, housing, and the environment. Greider notes that we allow the powerful to place a "screen" of distortions in front of us, behind which our two political parties, through "artful collusion," have "learned to work as one" on behalf of the powerful–their "clients."[1]

I believe that we, as a people, are incapable of attending to a significant and sustained public effort unless and until we can turn away from the distractions so that we may see through the "screen" of distortions. Only in the silence that follows can we create stores of vision and find within ourselves the necessary wisdom and strength. The silence can bring inspiration, truth, and a sure knowledge of who we are and why we're here.

It should be motivational to keep in mind that our mass entertainments are intended almost exclusively for commercial purposes. "They" want your money and have great trepidation that you may discover your mind. The fact that there is illness and mental impairment widespread in the population is not at all considered. Bottom lines and quarterly reports generate economic imperatives that send the distractions out and upon us, like hoards of pickpockets without conscience.

In our present state, we are thoroughly distracted and are treated largely as spending machines to be activated. As much as we may be proud of the Constitution of the United States, we are mostly indifferent to it and ignorant about it.[2] Contrary to James Madison's hopes,[3] our elected representatives who were to be bulwarks against the evil of factions, have let us down. With few exceptions, our representatives' brand of "wisdom" has allowed them to attend to their own interests before the interests of the country. In such a condition and impaired by toxins beyond our genetic potential, we must perform brilliantly as never before in order to keep the Earth a habitable planet for our children. Strength can come, if it ever does, from turning within and facing ourselves in the quiet.

Are we here in this life to watch our children sink into the mire of a brute world on a planet we've made treacherous and uninhabitable? What is our purpose? Who are we? What have we become? Only from the silence can answers that bring strength and hope be born. Samuel Johnson understood that thinking deeply about such things is heavy lifting for the mind and soul. He also understood a cure that would end the lethargy. He said, "Depend on it, sir. When a man knows he is to be hanged in a fortnight, it concentrates his mind wonderfully."[4] We are at that place. We must ready ourselves—in the quiet.

CHAPTER 12

OPTIMAL HEALTH

In addition to being distracted, Americans, in general, do not have optimal health. Optimal health is more than just the absence of an obvious disease. It involves having the strength to tear through difficult days, sustaining great efforts and large hopes. The effort to effectively institute use of the domestic violence clause will entail much strength, energy, and courage. An America saddled with ill health can not do it. We will need a populace in which optimal health is the rule rather than the exception. How that can be made to happen requires some thought about the major factor limiting our ability to reach optimal health.

At present, the most significant reason for our falling short of that goal is that the legal and regulatory structure of our society (laws and regulations dealing with the environment, agriculture, foods and drugs, etc.) tends to be *market based and not health based*. In other words, the laws and governmental actions, which should work as shields against harm, are driven by economics instead of being "human centered," as René Dubos would say. Allowing the meat and dairy industry, for example, to use growth hormones and antibiotics is, at best, sound in terms of short-run economics, but is sordid as public health policy. Your health is being traded away on a daily basis for someone's profit. Government, it seems, can readily get its arms around a simple economic concept. A complex human centered public health policy, however, hardly ever makes its way to center stage.

To use another example, salmon normally take three to four years to mature. Government now allows commercial fish farmers to accelerate growth and bring them to market in just ten to twelve months by permitting the use of a growth hormone obtained through genetic engineering.[1] The economics of it are simple; potential adverse human health consequences, however, are long and complex inquiries. The fact that the U. S. government allows that process to occur without first rectifying the obvious damage done to us from growth hormones in meat and dairy products points to the conclusion that allowing the use of growth hormones in genetically engineered salmon is merely a thoughtless continuation of the old policy: let simple economics dictate the course of what should instead be a long and complex effort at seeking human centered public health answers.

The fact that our governmental regulatory systems are not health based or human centered was made quite clear to me in 1981. That was the year that I, at age 42, entered state government service as an administrator enforcing compliance with environmental laws. My previous training had been strictly in the law. I was marvelously unburdened by preconceived judgments concerning technical and health issues.

One of the first problems that presented itself involved low levels of pollution detected in a private well that supplied water to twenty families. A decision had to be made as to whether those low levels posed a sufficient risk to require closing of the well. I asked the people who worked for me about how those toxins would be tolerated by children, the elderly, and pregnant women. What were the known long term effects on health and behavior of constant exposure to toxins at the particular levels? To my shock and surprise, no one could come anywhere near supplying competent answers to those questions. My staff had been trained as engineers. My state government department and the federal Environmental Protection Agency were created in the early 1970s and staffed almost exclusively with engineers. To this day, state and federal departments of health are not intimately involved with the health issues posed by toxins.

When I asked whether toxins in the well under consideration could bring about illness or harm the unborn and very young children, my enforcement group had no idea. Instead, they referred to certain cancer studies on some of the toxins. Those studies had almost nothing to do with the twenty families who were drinking from the well in question. The studies were done on mice which had been bred specifically to be susceptible to cancer. Every known carcinogen was then excluded from their environment except one, and that one was administered in massive, continuous doses. If the particular toxin then caused cancer in the mice, it could then be suspected of causing cancer in humans when ingested at some unknown, high enough, and continuing doses. *That was it*; that was essentially what environmental enforcement officers knew about whether the well should or should not be shut down.

It didn't take arduous training in the sciences to realize how far from reality the scientific community and the governmental regulatory officers had strayed. In the real world of those twenty families, each person was continually exposed to thousands of chemicals every day, from the toothpaste they used in the morning to the mercury in the paint on the walls behind them as they slept. Some of these exposures operated synergistically with one another, boosting their potential for harm by acting in concert with one another. Exposures that occurred years before may have been mutagenic, causing structural damage to a person's DNA. That individual could, as a result, have been made unusually susceptible to diseases caused by chemicals in the well at extremely low doses, acting as co-factors along with that person's damaged DNA. Some of the exposures, along with toxins in the water, might have been reaching a developing embryo or fetus with dreaded but unknown consequences.

To make matters even more complicated, it has been known from time immemorial that mood and outlook affect health. A broken heart is a stress that can break one's health. The loss of a loved one can bring death to the bereaved. Chemical exposures, if they do nothing else, directly affect mood, mental acuity, and outlook. Chemically induced torpor, therefore, diminishes mental outlook, which alone can bring about illness and further mental decline. Often, the illness gets directed to that person's unique place of physical weakness. Thus, for some the health failure will occur in the lungs or kidneys. For others, the heart or the skeletal structure is the weakest link. The connection between a toxin and a resulting condition of ill health is hardly ever established.

In the face of such daunting complexity, the mice studies are almost totally irrelevant. Yet, the governmental regulatory system often ordered that they be done. Industry paid for them. In the end, they proved little and took us all very far afield of what was going on in the real world. Just looking at the decision making process involved in closing that one well, I came to understand how government failed us. Because cancer is a readily observable and countable event in both animals and humans, it became just about the sole object for governmental decision making. Lack of optimal health is the general condition of the population because, in large part, our laws and the regulatory agencies just could not be made to focus on complex health based questions.

I left government service in 1982, less than two years after taking the position, stunned by so much of what I had witnessed. I started to study health and environmental issues. In 1983, I began an effort to warn people and find like-minded souls. A letter was published in which I noted that we are experiencing general ill health in our population. The health decline, I said, was being brought about, in large part, by toxins, which were causing malaise, depression, and were sapping the strength Americans would need to keep democracy working.[2] No one responded to the letter.

In 1984, I shared a public platform with a physician who had previously been an administrator with the EPA in charge of their risk assessment program. I took the position that toxins were having a deleterious effect on Americans, both physically (in a subclinical way) and behaviorally. I suggested that government ought to regulate in such a way that those harms be eliminated. The former risk assessment officer did not disagree that we were being affected in such a subtle manner. From his experience in government, however, he did not believe it could be accomplished. Doing so, he said, "would be far too complex."[3] Of course, the doctor did not mean "too complex" in a medical or scientific sense. He only meant that sufficient financial resources were not likely to be available to accomplish a human centered governmental public health effort. He was correct. Only through a restructuring of priorities under the domestic violence clause can government be compelled to change focus and make commonplace what could not formerly have even been imagined.

Many people in government are aware that the near exclusive focus on cancer has been shortsighted. According to the Congressional Office of Technology Assessment, the adverse effects of toxic chemicals "on organs and organ systems, particularly the nervous system, may pose an equal or greater threat to public health." Commenting on that observation, then Senator Albert Gore, Jr., chairman of the Subcommittee on Science, Technology, and Space, added: "Chronic neurotoxicity presents a health risk every bit as large and as tragic as cancer, yet almost nothing is being done about it. Our regulatory system is virtually blind to this risk."[4] Dr. Ila L. Cote, of EPA's Office of Research and Development, likened the fact that we don't monitor toxins for noncancer health risks as being "like the guy who only looks under the light to find his keys, when he knows he has dropped them outside the light."[5]

Creating a thorough and efficient, all encompassing health based environmental regulatory system is what the domestic violence clause was designed to do. Optimal health is, in a sense, the birthright the framers had in mind for us. Certainly, they would view with utter disdain continuous government involvement in the setting up and maintaining of an economics centered regulatory system that actually brings about ill health and diminution of human potential. Use of the domestic violence clause can end the terrible environmental harms that we visit upon ourselves and one another.

In the meantime, the present governmental regulatory structure allows and encourages continuing exposures to a myriad of toxins. These are considerable vectors of ill health, acting as a weight upon us. In order for us to begin gathering sufficient strength to mount a people's effort to initiate and oversee use of the domestic violence clause, we will have to undertake personal campaigns to purify as much as possible our own environments and our own diets. We will have to personally monitor and eliminate as many exposures to toxins as is humanly possible.

The biblical story of Samson's prenatal and childhood care[6] is amazingly analogous to our present circumstances. An angel of the Lord appeared to the wife of Manoah and told her she would soon conceive a child who was to be a Nazirite or servant unto God *from the womb* to the day of his death. Accordingly, Manoah's wife was cautioned, even before conception, to avoid wine and strong drink. Further, she was not to eat anything "unclean." Hebrew dietary laws, on which that latter obligation was based, would have ensured that Samson's meat was fresh and taken from herbivores exclusively. It would tend to be parasite free and without any signs of disease. What seafood was eaten would have come from surface and not bottom dwellers.[7] In this way was Samson to be made strong so that he could carry out his mission in life. According to the angel of the Lord, Samson was to "begin" to save or deliver Israel out of the hand of the Philistines.[8]

We must be an army of Samsons with sufficient wisdom and courage, this time, to deliver us from ourselves. The way to strengthen ourselves, getting us to optimal health, is through diligent adherence to advice similar to what the angel of the Lord told Samson's mother. Many have already started the cleansing and purifying process on the road to optimal health.

CHAPTER 13

THE ROAD TO OPTIMAL HEALTH

Intuitively, knowing there is a major challenge ahead, a good number of people are preparing by getting on the road to optimal health. They appreciate that our bodies were designed to move and bend and lift and stretch. They do it all and they do it often, finding exercise programs that suit their need to build strength and stamina.

Many are turning off television and radio and turning them back on only for an occasional entertainment or a program that fills a real personal need. Those small acts are giant steps in the direction of optimal health. The steady diet of advertising, violence, inane chatter, and managed news keep us from the stillness within that is our wellspring of mental and physical health.

More and more people are visiting that wellspring, even in a busy day, by taking time for meditation or prayer. Some do it by guiding themselves into a quiet inner place with a book or a favorite poem. Others do it with a select piece of music. Such practices are paths to the stillness that is sometimes called "pure consciousness" and "spiritual awareness." Being on those paths not only makes one physically stronger, but thinking and feeling capacities are enhanced.[1]

At the stores, many of us are turning away from products that contain toxins and are buying, instead, products that are harmless and natural. We have lost many freedoms. Much of what presently stands for political liberty is simply a hollow exercise, a touting of form over substance. But we still have the power, as consumers, to select what *we* wish to use, wear, eat, and drink. Each decision to purify ourselves helps to inform and transform the marketplace. Accordingly, every such step has a curative effect upon both the self and upon society.

Following the above regimens and using harmless, natural products is likely to give a person exuberant energy. We will need every bit of that energy to accomplish the task of putting the domestic violence clause to work. Toxins act as dead weight, holding us back.

As René Dubos might have put it, our bodies were designed to run on pure water only. We have no God-given filtering mechanism to keep out the toxic chemicals that are now endemic to our water systems. We will have to take inordinate care to make sure that the water we use for drinking, cooking, and bathing is as untainted as possible. Using only pure water can have instant health dividends. Many people are finding that their immune systems are boosted by continued use of pure water.

Our lungs have no filter mechanism to keep out the modern chemical poisons in the air we breathe, which has been aptly termed, not just air pollution but "toxic fallout."[2] The best the body can do is to lift offensive materials that have been deposited in the lungs and carry them, like a bucket brigade, up the trachea so that they can be expelled with a cough or a sneeze. This lifting and carrying is done by the specialized cilia processes—minute hairlike structures that beat in rhythmic waves, moving particles of pollution up and out of the lungs.

The cilia, however, do not work while one is smoking. Poisons in cigarette smoke as well as the witches' brew of toxins in the air then get trapped together in the lungs. Constantly clearing the lungs of lodged toxins without cilial action becomes the full time work of one's internal immune system. People so burdened are likely to have less energy for the important work ahead. They are also more likely to be disabled by resulting illnesses. Giving up smoking and other such risks is more than a personal challenge. Quitting is a benefit to us all, and great efforts to help those who are addicted ought to be made.

In less threatening times, society could afford the luxury of having large numbers of people turn to disabling behavior like smoking, drugs, and alcohol dependency. Now, things are quite different. The world is like a sinking ship that is taking on water. Its working crew is far too small in number to keep up with the inflow of seawater. Those who sit in deck chairs, disabled by their own destructive behavior, are desperately needed to function effectively as members of the crew.

Jane and Richard Cicchetti are founders of the Five Elements Center in Mountain Lakes, New Jersey, a place for the study of holistic and gentle healing arts. Jane once said something about our skin that would have made René Dubos proud: "Don't put anything on your skin that you would not use as dressing for your salad." Her comment was incisive. Our skins, made for gentler times, are porous. What goes on can also go right into the body. Yet our skin has become a major focus for the chemical industry in advertising and for moving products into the home market. Many people are now thinking twice before continuing to use unnecessary chemicals for the skin and hair. Ongoing exposures in chemical soaps, sprays, shampoos, conditioners, etc., can be significant.

For washing, so many people are just using soap. Pure soap is simply a plant or animal fat, mixed with an alkali, usually ashes from plant material. There are also fine natural shampoos with no additional chemical additives, other than natural oils or herbs. Chemicals used for personal hygiene are an unnecessary source of exposures to toxins brought into the home market for a thoughtless profit that will tend to keep us from optimal health.

Clean skin and true radiant beauty are fostered from within, as well. Nothing works better than eating plenty of organic fruits, vegetables, and grains. A lot of people who eat meat are demanding that it should be organic and free of hormones. Many are skipping all refined sugar (cakes, pies, cookies) and eat dairy products sparingly, if at all. Organic eggs are now widely available. Salt shakers are being used less by those who are getting to know the tastes of various herbs and spices, many of which have healing properties. As health and strength build, the need for stimulants like caffeine fades.

In the fall, leaves are being gathered, not discarded, to be put into a compost pile. Tree roots go deep into the earth and take up minerals that find their way into the leaves. Soil enriched by that compost allows us to grow our own vegetables and fruits that are rich in the necessary vitamins and minerals. Preserving, canning, and freezing are easy ways to store a bounty of healthful foods. More and more Americans are doing just that.

Cleaning the house and keeping it pest free need not result in chemical exposures. Natural products like baking soda, borax, salt, distilled white vinegar, lemon juice, sparing use of TSP (made from soda ash, phosphoric acid, and caustic soda), and some ingenuity can make one's house safe and clean without ill effects.[3]

As people keep to these regimens, illness tends to be rare in their lives. When it comes, however, they do not immediately smother the symptoms with over-the-counter and prescription medicines. Illness is instructive, a way for the body to tell us of changes that need to be made in nutrition and in lifestyle. A growing number of people now prepare for healing and strengthening of body and spirit by learning about herbal remedies, homeopathy, and a wide array of natural aids to healthy living. Until his or her education becomes more respectful of these gentle approaches, your medical doctor may not be considered the final word on how to get to optimal health or even how best to treat an illness.[4]

The use of pesticides, fungicides, and chemical fertilizers on lawns is a dangerous short cut encouraged by chemical companies to continue sales into the home market. About a fifth of the 1.08 billion pounds of pesticides used each year go to the non farm market.[5] Organic substitutes exist.[6] Better still, consider the wise counsel of Sara Stein, author of *Noah's Garden*.[7] She correctly characterizes our yards and gardens as a "vast, nearly continuous, and terribly impoverished ecosystem for which we ourselves, with our mowers, shears, and misguided choice of plants are responsible."[8] The chemical lawn, she says is "cut off from the life support systems on which the natural survival of grass depends, and it must therefore remain permanently in intensive care."[9] Her argument in favor of creating an ecosystem on our properties that "we and every other creature need" for survival is, I believe, rather compelling.[10] After reading *Noah's Garden*, you may be moved to return your area of this country into a working, complex ecosystem.

People that I have known who have begun to travel this road to optimal health are different from their former selves. Surely, they are thinner and look better. Yes, they tend to have more energy; they are not often ill. But, beyond all that, they seem to acquire something else. They are spiritually lighter. Mixed with their determination is an ample measure of both humor and perspective. And as they purify themselves, each act also purifies the world with their wisdom.

CHAPTER 14

COMMUNITY

I have already mentioned the need to find a way through our present condition of environmental domestic violence by experiencing silence. Individually, in the quiet, we can begin to assemble bits of knowledge and wisdom. I hold, however, with Samuel Johnson, that "the end of learning is piety,"[1] which, to Johnson, meant service as much as reverence. With all the strength and clarity we can muster, we should reach out (as I am doing to you) to each other. Knowledge and wisdom can be put into service as we connect with one another. Change, if it is to arrive in the time that it must, requires community discussion and community action. We have to do it ourselves. Counting so heavily on the "patriotism and love of justice" of our elected representatives, as did James Madison,[2] has been a disappointment.

These proposed public discussions should have a unifying theme upon which to focus critical attention. I suggest using the words "Article Four," because the domestic violence clause is located in Article IV, Section 4 of the Constitution. In this way, Article Four meetings can offer an opportunity to individuals and groups who are suffering injury from environmental domestic violence and can allow all to gather for discussion in the same place. The coming together of persons and groups with a common grievance is the necessary first step to the solution of that grievance.

If you are trying to rid your schools and your neighborhoods of lead contamination, you have an Article Four problem. That is a harm we have done to ourselves. If you have a child with cancer, you have an Article Four problem. Before we polluted the Earth, children didn't get cancer in the great numbers we are seeing today. If you or a loved one has breast cancer, you have an Article Four problem. That epidemic is peculiar to the chemical age we've created. According to the framers' conceptual understanding of domestic violence, any person who has experienced or is experiencing physical harm or property damage as a result of our environmental heedlessness, has an Article Four problem as long as the resolution is beyond the police powers of the states. States can't even begin to deal effectively with such plagues as existing lead pollution and the turning around of epidemic increases in cancer. Those problems require a cohesive national policy and continuous adequate funding to reduce the exposures that are so sorely affecting us.

If you suffer from one of the growing number of chronic health problems, you should find your way to an Article Four meeting. The combination of continuing exposures to toxins and a chemically degraded food supply simply insures the existence of chronic health problems in the population. More and more, researchers are linking diseases to genetic defects. While, at first blush, one would think that a genetic defect had nothing to do with an environmental factor, the very opposite is true. Chemical exposures cause genetic defects that then predispose an individual to various diseases. If you or a loved one has an ailment that is thought to be linked to a genetic weakness, you have an Article Four problem.

In like manner, if you are drug or alcohol dependent, that dependence was either caused or made worse by environmental toxins. You have an Article Four problem. If you are dyslexic or have difficulties computing or thinking, Article Four is of interest to you. If you have experienced in yourself or your loved ones a marked lack of self control or motivation, Article Four needs to be addressed.

Certainly, if you are a teacher, or involved with health care, or are part of the criminal justice system, you are seeing the effects of environmental domestic violence daily. Your involvement at Article Four meetings can make it possible to bring education to a new effectiveness, get people well again, and stop the wasting of so much human potential in our jails and in our criminal courts.

Almost without exception, you care deeply about this lovely Earth and its inhabitants. If I can generalize, the more you care and fear for their loss, the more you've held the present political parties in disdain for not offering hope. Article Four meetings are the answer for you.

You may wish to begin the process of coming together in community by first reading Article IV, Section 4 to yourself. It belongs to *you*. The framers had you in mind when they wrote it. The United States is obligated to you: it must protect you from the harm we have ended up doing to ourselves and to one another.

If you are directly affected by environmental exposures or understand how close we are to the brink of disaster, just call a few people whom you believe are similarly affected or are of a similar belief. Get together and just start talking about the problem. Don't be put off by what experts may say. *This is your clause. It's your country.* There are precious few experts who are not in the pay of the economic interests that have helped to create the problem. Meet often. Widen the circle of people involved. Quite literally, the fate of our species and the fate of this planet are in our hands right now.

When we gather to talk, it will be much like a family trying to figure its way out of difficulties. We have all been shortsighted about so many important things. It would be best to forgive one another so that we can go on from here. Environmental laws have done little more than pit brother against brother in an endless array of wasteful legal battles. Now, as caring members of one family, we can begin the healing process inherent in careful use of the domestic violence clause.

You will find yourselves dealing with some very interesting concepts. Chief among them is what exact role are you to play in the process. The shaping of policy and procedures under the domestic violence clause is an example of direct democracy in action. You, not the people you voted for, are to define the terms to ensure survival. What the phrase means and how it is to be implemented are up to you.

CHAPTER 15

SWORDS INTO PLOWSHARES[1]

Your Article Four discussions are likely to take you quickly to the cost of implementing a total mobilization under the domestic violence clause. Costs will be measured in the trillions of dollars. Where will that money come from? I propose that it comes from the stopping of wasteful spending and the dedication of those funds to Article Four needs.

Clearly, the single largest item in the public budget that can be drastically cut and so dedicated is the cost of our military. We do *not* live in a dangerous world that requires such expenditures. Foreign risks that presently exist were actually created by our senseless military positions over the last fifty years. The few dangers that we face can be ameliorated politically, and the trillions of dollars we save must be used to assure survival from the real threat of environmental domestic violence.

Where and when did we veer off course so dramatically? The place was Washington, D. C., and the time was 1946. We initiated a senseless military overreaction that escalated into the Cold War. There can be no progress in redirecting our public monies into peaceful and useful efforts unless and until we analyze and understand the Cold War for the wasteful error that it was.

In 1945, Russia emerged from the devastation of World War II intact but thoroughly incapable of waging war against the Western Powers. U. S. chargé d'affaires George Kennan, in his now famous "Long Telegram" sent to the U. S. State Department on February 22, 1946, informed Washington that: "Gauged against [the] Western world as a whole, [the] Soviets are still by far the weaker force."[2] Nor, according to Kennan, did Russia have war in mind. As he put it, "In international economic matters, Soviet policy will really be dominated by [the] pursuit of autarchy for [the] Soviet Union and [the] Soviet-dominated adjacent areas taken together." Thus, according to Kennan, "I think it possible [that] Soviet foreign trade may be restricted largely to [the] Soviet's own security sphere, including [the] occupied areas in Germany, and that a cold shoulder may be turned to [the] principle of general economic collaboration among nations."[3] Russia, in other words, was turning *inward*. It was looking to establish absolute sovereignty over its own territories; it wanted to create a self sufficient and independent national economy.

The significance of the Kennan Long Telegram should not be underestimated.[4] Even though it confirmed that Russia did not wish to make war, it triggered our embarking on a reckless spiral of Cold War carnage and spending. What did George Kennan perceive in that backward, recluse Russia which caused him to cable on February 22, 1946, with "such urgent importance,"[5] that the Soviet threat "should be approached with [the] same thoroughness and care as [the] solution of [a] major strategic problem in war and, if necessary, with no smaller outlay in planning effort"?[6]

Kennan, in fact, was mainly reacting to a *speech* recently made by Premier Josef Stalin that was, in essence and according to Kennan, identical to a 1927 speech he had given "to a delegation of American workers," during which Stalin had said:

> In the course of further development of international revolution there will emerge two centers of world significance: a socialist center, drawing to itself the countries which tend toward socialism, and a capitalist center, drawing to itself the countries that incline toward capitalism. [The] battle between these two centers for command of [the] world economy will decide [the] fate of capitalism and of communism in the entire world.[7]

To that old challenge, Stalin added that internal conflicts and wars were inherent in capitalism; if Russia just remained independent and militarily strong, those conflicts between capitalist states, although potentially dangerous to Russia, could result in advancement of the socialist cause.[8]

These were hardly fighting words. To the contrary, they were words involving an *openly* expressed challenge from one economic system to another. The Soviets believed that all property should be collectively or communally owned (communism). They faulted our system whereby private individuals could own property (capitalism). There is no question that in 1946 Russia intended to preach its message to the world. There is also no question that Russia did *not* intend to take its message to the world by use of the sword.

The only difference between 1927 and 1946 was that Russia now existed as a large, permanent, and well recognized nation with a clear potential for effectively drawing to itself the countries that would "tend toward socialism." In that way, it was indeed a "center" in the battle "for command of the world economy." This was the recurring nightmare come true of American interests with a continuing desire to control natural resources and markets abroad.

In theory, communism would deny the right of individuals to own property and to direct the energy of workers. In theory, all peoples of the Earth would share the bounty of its offering. Communism, as envisioned by Karl Marx and Friedrich Engels in 1848, was Christianity itself dressed up as economics. To owners of property it was anathema. One could all too easily, so they feared, confuse religious-like sentiments with "real-world" economics, which they felt required private ownership.

To appreciate the underlying fear that was fueled by George Kennan's Long Telegram, one need only recall what the United States attempted to do in Russia between 1918 and 1921. That chapter in American history is not often discussed and is treated dismissively by those who feel they must mention it.[9] Once again, Russia had been at war with Germany, with devastating consequences to itself. It has been estimated that over half of all Russian soldiers mobilized were killed, wounded, or taken prisoner.[10] The end of World War I brought both victory over Germany and the overthrow of Nicholas II, Tsar of Russia, in 1917 by the Bolsheviks, a movement that embraced communism. The United States had no particular affection for Tsar Nicholas II, nor for the tsarist, monarchical government. Certainly, the Bolsheviks, now leaders over a war-torn nation, were no military threat to Europe. Nevertheless, because it was the first communist government, we attempted to murder this infant in its first hours.

In 1918, the United States, along with fourteen other countries, including Germany, invaded Russia and participated in a civil war against the Bolsheviks. That war lasted for three years with severe Russian casualties and dislocations. Foreign invasion forces consisted of some 160,000 troops, well supplied with advanced weaponry.[11] In 1921, the communists prevailed and were left with the sure knowledge that their very existence constituted a threat to the Western powers, allies or not.

In 1946, there were essentially two ways to meet Russia's challenge to the ethics of capitalism, the high road and the low road. The high road was expressed by Britain's chargé d'affaires in Moscow, Frank Roberts, by a cable to the British Foreign Minister dated March 18, 1946. Roberts suggested that the best approach was to pursue, both at home and abroad, progressive policies that would raise the standard of living of people and remove "the causes of social strife. At the same time we can offer civil and personal liberties which are unknown in the Soviet Union and would be the envy of its inhabitants. In fact, we should act as the champions of a dynamic and progressive faith and way of life with an appeal to the World at least as great as that of the Communist system of the Kremlin." In such well tended soil, said Roberts, communism was unlikely to spread.[12]

We, on the other hand, embarked on the low road. As pointed out by the noted historian, Henry Steele Commager, we attempted to eradicate, both at home and abroad, even the thought of communism.[13] With stunning quickness, the American government met Russia's *words* with actual preparations for war. We, unilaterally and without justification, started the Cold War in a few short months following receipt of George Kennan's Long Telegram.

Just how our anti-Soviet frenzy moved the Russians to conclude, in 1946, that they were in peril can now be more clearly understood, owing to the Novikov cable, a document newly discovered in the archives of the Soviet Foreign Ministry.[14] It was published in 1991 in *Origins of the Cold War* by the United States Institute of Peace, an independent federal institution founded by Congress whose aim is to promote the peaceful resolution of international conflict.[15] Its editor, Kenneth M. Jensen, noted that "by and large, the facts and events cited by Novikov were a matter of public knowledge at the time" and can be readily verified by any "interested reader."[16]

On September 27, 1946, just seven months after George Kennan's Long Telegram, Nikolai Novikov, Soviet Ambassador to the United States, sent a cable to Foreign Minister Viacheslav Molotov from Washington, D. C. Novikov described an abrupt shift in the foreign policy of the United States from cooperation to confrontation and said that the conservatives were now in full control of that policy.[17] He related that in the summer of 1946, "for the first time in the history of the country," Congress enacted a peacetime draft. The army was to number about one million persons in July of 1947, and the Navy was to be near its World War II strength.[18] Military expenditures "have risen colossally," said Novikov, being more than ten times greater than expenditures in 1938 and approaching 40 percent of the 1946-1947 budget of 36 billion dollars. The United States was in the process of planning for and building 486 naval and air bases, points of support, and radio stations across the Atlantic and Pacific Oceans.[19]

Novikov said further: "How far the policy of the American government has gone with regard to China is indicated by the fact that at present it is striving to effect control over China's army. Recently the U. S. administration submitted to Congress a bill on military assistance to China that provided for the complete reorganization of the Chinese army, its training with the aid of U. S. military instructors, and its supply with American weapons and equipment."[20] Molotov's copy of the cable shows that he, Molotov, put two vertical lines in the margin adjacent to the above sentences plus an exclamation point, also in the margin.[21]

American intentions with regard to this buildup of force, as cabled by Novikov, were being made clear by President Truman and other leaders. They asserted, "that the United States has the right to lead the world. All forces of American diplomacy–the army, the air force, the navy, industry, and science–are enlisted in the service of this foreign policy." The military expansion was to be "implemented ...through the *arms race*, and through the creation of *ever newer types of weapons*."[22] (emphasis added)

Novikov further reported that a campaign was under way to "create an atmosphere of war psychosis" among the people. "American government, political, and military figures" were making "extremely hostile statements...with regard to the Soviet Union and its foreign policy.... These statements are echoed in an even more unrestrained tone by the overwhelming majority of the American press organs. Talk about...a war against the Soviet Union, and even a direct call for this war–with the threat of using the atomic bomb– such is the content of the statements...by reactionaries at public meetings and in the press." Nor, said Novikov, was such "preaching war...a monopoly of the far right." The "yellow American press"– Hearst and McCormick, as well as the "reputable and respectable" *New York Times* and *New York Herald Tribune* joined in as well. Novikov cited the most respected American columnist of the day, Walter Lippmann, as "almost undisguisedly" calling "on the United States to launch a strike against the Soviet Union in the most vulnerable areas of the south and southeast of the USSR."[23]

Novikov concluded that the United States was preparing "for a future war...against the Soviet Union," which it considered was "the main obstacle in the path of the United States to world domination."[24] Molotov and the Russian government could conclude nothing less. The Cold War, just months after receipt of Kennan's Long Telegram, was already careening out of control.

At that exact time, much of the Third World was in the process of throwing off controls over their sovereignty imposed by the European empires.[25] President Roosevelt and his diverse coalition of leadership recognized an obligation to honor their rights for self-determination.[26] In that regard and for a short time, the United States had been able to stand apart from the Europeans and reflect a sincere respect for the freedom of all nations to define their own cultures and control their own economics.[27] But the Truman administration's "global crusade against Communists"[28] turned the hopes of the colonized world into a "negligible factor" as America rushed about the world propping up the weakened European colonial powers.[29]

"Anticommunism replaced proselytizing the American dream as fundamental policy." We "stumbled blindly" into a host of military interventions, "violently toppling" foreign governments if we feared disloyalty.[30] Unaligned, nationalist movements in the Third World were often treated little better than communist inspired movements.[31] We preferred imperial ties and oligopolies as "spokes of stability."[32] All the while, we poured out a continuing stream of hate images upon the Russians which were easily adapted from America's attitudes toward the Japanese in World War II. Accordingly, the Russians were supposedly capable of, as historian John Dower listed, "deviousness and cunning, bestial and atrocious behavior, homogeneity and monolithic control, fanaticism divorced from any legitimate goals or realistic perceptions of the world, [and] megalomania bent on world conquest."[33]

Historians Melvin Gurtov and Ray Maghoori, in their 1984 book, *Roots of Failure*, neatly summed up the one sided nature of the Cold War and where responsibility for that war lies:

> Soviet behavior in world affairs has aimed at expanding its influence and its margin of security. But the Russians can not be held solely or even primarily responsible for the character of U. S. foreign policy. U. S. policy has sought to satisfy the economic, political, psychological, and bureaucratic needs of particular groups and persons within the United States as much as it has attempted to contain or to eliminate external threats to the nation's well-being. Indeed, those needs, which are usually hidden in appeals to protect the national interest, have become so compelling that they, rather than any foreign military establishment or ideology, pose the most immediate threats to human security in this country and abroad.

The Third World remains an object of U. S. foreign policy for the extraction of profit, valuable resources, and military vantage points...This is understandable in light of the frequently cited fact that the United States, with about 5 percent of the world's population, consumes over 30 percent of the world's product. Such a voracious appetite creates foreign-policy 'imperatives,' such as intervention to ensure 'stability,' and 'vital interests,' such as secure access to sources of energy....[34]

In accord is Howard Zinn, who wrote in *A People's History of the United States*:

...When, right after the war, the American public, war-weary, seemed to favor demobilization and disarmament, the Truman administration (Roosevelt had died in April 1945) worked to create an atmosphere of crisis and cold war. True, the rivalry with the Soviet Union was real–that country had come out of the war with its economy wrecked and 20 million dead, but was making an astounding comeback, rebuilding its industry, regaining military strength. The Truman administration, however, presented the Soviet Union as not just a rival but *an immediate threat*. (emphasis added)

In a series of moves abroad and at home, it established a climate of fear–a hysteria about Communism–which would steeply escalate the military budget and stimulate the economy with war-related orders. This combination of policies would permit more aggressive actions abroad, more repressive actions at home.[35]

The Cold War that brought death and destruction to the world was a fantasy woven out of deceits for the purpose of corporate profits. It diminished all who felt its wrath, and it diminished us. We can no longer even imagine a peaceful world. Those who imposed the Cold War upon us took away the better part of our souls.

Speaking only of publicly budgeted dollars and excluding the cost of veterans' benefits as well as interest on the national debt, U. S. military spending from 1948 projected through 1995 has been meticulously compiled by the Center for Defense Information in Washington, D. C. Adjusted for inflation in 1994 dollars, the amount we wasted on the Cold War is over 13.6 trillion dollars.[36] Use of that money for human and environmental protection could have assured survival and spared us the indignities of disease and behavioral decline.

A proposal for some steps to demilitarize our nation is contained in the next chapter.

CHAPTER 16

EARTHCEDING

If your Article Four discussions are like the ones I've seen, surely, some people will be aghast at the suggestion of demilitarizing the United States to all but a Coast Guard and some reserve units. We live in a dangerous world, they say, and need to be well armed because of leaders like the Ayatollah Khomeini and Saddam Hussein. Although threats of that sort are usually overstated, there is some need to protect ourselves against them, nevertheless. The error is in believing that our security can only be maintained by continuous combat readiness. The very opposite is true.

We are like the farmer who sees that his family and his animals have begun to sicken and his barn has begun to burn, yet goes to town to buy bullets and a new gun. There might indeed be a justifiable need for the farmer to buy weapons, but not when illness and conflagration require all of his energies and resources.

On a worldwide scale, evidence continues to mount that we have damaged the Earth's protective ozone layer[1] and have started a global warming trend.[2] The percentage of carbon dioxide and other greenhouse gases is rising and the level of oxygen in the air we breathe is falling.[3] The potential consequences of just these items is devastation beyond our imaginations.

Jacques Cousteau, now in his 80s, has spent a lifetime studying the world's oceans and rivers. So frightened of the degradation we have brought about, he says, "I'm now fighting for my own species. I finally understood that we ourselves are in danger."[4]

Third World governments are no match for international business interests that are destroying rain forests[5] and farms.[6] Air pollution threatens inhabitants from Mexico City[7] to Patancheru, India,[8] as businesses rush to produce in countries of least regulation and low wages. Everywhere there are the dangerous wastes of all that activity seeping into groundwaters and entering the food chain for world distribution. Life support systems of this precious planet are crumbling under the weight of our present abuse, and the Earth's population is growing by an unprecedented billion people every ten years.[9]

Responding to those who want to maintain a large standing army for protection against the Khomeinis and the Husseins, are we not like the farmer who should be tending to the crisis at hand? We're just not used to accepting the truth of our present environmental plight. We soothe ourselves by an artful denial.[10] In fact, we face unprecedented environmental perils. New forms of crisis demand new thinking. Security by the use of weapons is old thinking. Abraham Lincoln expressed the need for new thinking most aptly in his 1862 Message to Congress. He proposed emancipation of slaves as a step toward peace during the Civil War in these words:

> The dogmas of the quiet past are inadequate to the stormy present. The occasion is piled high with difficulty, and we must rise with the occasion. As our case is new, *so must we think anew.* We must disenthrall ourselves, and then we shall save our country.[11] (emphasis added)

Thinking through things anew, it appears clear to me that we must focus on the error our country made in 1946. At that time, out of fear of communism, we interfered with the process of allowing nations to determine for themselves what their form of government and what their economic priorities would be. Local people know infinitely better than outside interests how to care for and protect their part of the Earth. Chico Mendez knew better than the cattle industry and the international food supply companies the best uses of his beloved Amazon rain forest.[12] As a *first principle*, complete economic and political independence must be granted to individual nations and the indigenous peoples. That takes no weapons to accomplish. In fact, much of the world's weaponry is presently being used to suppress efforts of the Third World nations and indigenous peoples to protect themselves and their natural resources.

Since the United States is the only remaining superpower, with the military capability of striking at will any target in the world, something more than words is needed to bring about "self determination" throughout the world. Only the giving up, the ceding of those weapons, for the sake of the Earth and its inhabitants will do. Call it "Earthceding." In no other way can another nation's right to self determination be seriously considered as a true option by its people. Only then might they, for example, dare to distribute land to peasants or refuse to dam up a healthy and productive river system. Earthceding is hardly an option. Without it, endless destruction of habitat and resources will continue unabated.

Earthceding, the giving up of prerogatives so that the Earth will remain habitable, is important for another reason. Nations, like individuals, have souls that must be purged of guilt for harms brought about. We do a disservice to ourselves and the world by holding to the simple and false belief that we "won" the Cold War. With our arms and our power, we have devastated whole societies and have set holocausts in motion that continue to take lives to this day. Earthceding will allow us to face what we've done, ask for forgiveness, and proceed in brotherhood with peoples of the world.

For example, I propose that we ask forgiveness and mourn the death of Salvador Allende, the former president of Chile, whose assassination on September 11, 1973 was a consequence of our Cold War interferences with Chile's right to self determination. The Allende story is very much like what we've done throughout the world. Details about the matter are therefore instructive to illustrate these patterns of our conduct elsewhere.

An excellent and unbiased biography of Salvadore Allende was published in *Current Biography 1971.*[13] Born in 1908, Allende came from a Chilean family known for public service. One of his grandfathers, a physician, during military conflict organized the medical services of the Chilean army. Another founded the country's first secular school. Allende volunteered for military service after completing his secondary schooling at age sixteen and later earned an officer's rank in the army reserve. He graduated from medical school in 1932, having excelled in his studies. He later served as president of the Chilean Medical Association, president of the Pan-American Medical Conference, Chairman of the College of Physicians, and editor of the *Boletin medico de Chile* and *Medicina social*.

In 1933, Allende, as *Current Biography* relates, "along with other prominent leftists, founded the Socialist party of Chile as an alternative for Marxists who objected to the Communist party's rigid adherence to Soviet policies." He was first elected, as a socialist, to the Chilean Chamber of Deputies in 1937 and was first elected to the Senate in 1945. He was vice president of the Senate and served as its president from 1965 to 1969.

According to *Current Biography*, "during his long career as a legislator, he initiated over 100 bills, most of them dealing with public health, social welfare, and woman's rights." As Minister of Health, "he was also responsible for reforms in the government's social insurance program and in the industrial safety laws."

He ran for president of the country four times: 1951, 1958, 1964, and 1970. In 1970, Allende received a plurality but not a majority of the votes. Therefore, the Chilean Congress, which was not dominated by socialists and communists, had to vote for or against Allende as being appropriate for the presidency. He reassured all that his government would be "a nationalist, popular, *democratic*, and revolutionary government that will move toward socialism" in a manner "that fits Chilean reality." (emphasis added) To secure election in the Congress, Allende "agreed to the adoption of ten constitutional amendments designed to safeguard freedom of political parties, labor unions, civic associations, and the communications media, and an educational system free from political interference."

With those assurances given, he won 153 out of the 200 congressional votes and was inaugurated president on November 3, 1970. Allende pledged to "maintain the integrity and independence" of Chile. He implemented a land reform program begun by his predecessor whereby some of the large estates were converted into farm cooperatives. He nationalized selected industries and introduced a constitutional amendment in December of 1970 that would give the government "the right to the nation's mineral wealth, with considerable leeway in determining compensation. The amendment was unanimously passed by both houses of Congress" and signed by Allende in July of 1971.

His death by assassination during a bloody military coup on September 11, 1973 was not the expressed will of the Chilean people. Allende was murdered as a result of secret plottings done in your name for which you must begin to take responsibility, even if those people directly involved will not. President Nixon, after leaving office, showed no regret. "Hell, what was done in Chile," he said, "had to be done...there are some things the CIA has to be free to do."[14]

No statement better typifies this nation's out of control Cold War mentality than Henry Kissinger's words in June of 1970 to a high level CIA oversight committee. He was speaking on behalf of President Nixon as Assistant to the President for National Security Affairs. The business of the meeting was to determine what secret actions should be taken to prevent the election of Salvadore Allende in September. Kissinger implored the group with: "I don't see why we need to stand by and watch a country go Communist due to the irresponsibility of its own people."[15]

Between 1963 and 1973, the CIA, in close cooperation with a number of American companies doing business internationally, spent some $13.4 million on secret activities aimed at preventing Allende's election and destabilizing his government following the election. Companies involved included the International Telephone and Telegraph Corporation (ITT) and Anaconda Copper.[16] In an effort to bring about economic collapse of the Allende regime, the Nixon Administration cut off most economic assistance, discouraged private lines of credit, and blocked loans by international organizations.[17] President Nixon's direct and secret order to his CIA director, Richard Helms, was "...make the economy scream."[18]

While secret economic warfare was going on, Henry Kissinger, in September of 1970, said at a *public* press conference that Allende's Marxist regime would contaminate Argentina, Bolivia, and Peru. His comment was an artful use of the familiar Cold War domino theory intended to inflate the fearful significance of benign events.[19] In this case, it was more. It was the most powerful foreign affairs representative of the United States saying to the world that the United States considered Allende a direct threat. In the context of Cold War events in South and Central America, Kissinger's speech was the placement of a bounty upon the life of Salvadore Allende.

In or about that same month, September of 1970, an internal report of ITT was circulating. The eight page document, marked "personal and confidential," said that the American ambassador to Chile had received the "green light to move in the name of President Nixon...[with] maximum authority to do all possible–short of a Dominican Republic-type action–to keep Allende from taking power." It stated that the Chilean army "has been assured full material and financial assistance by the U. S. military establishment" and that ITT had "pledged [its financial] support if needed" to the anti-Allende forces.[20]

On September 11, 1973, while the Chilean economy was beset by inflation, strikes, food shortages, and international credit problems, Salvadore Allende was overthrown and killed in a coup carried out by members of the Chilean armed services and the national police.[21] Who actually engineered the final coup may never be known. CIA director William Colby, however, admitted that the CIA "had some intelligence coverage about the various moves being made," had "penetrated" all of Chile's major political parties, and secretly furnished "some assistance" to certain Chilean groups.[22] The United States set up in 1949 and maintains a "School of the Americas" in the Canal Zone where we train foreign military officers. The school is a hub of information to and from its graduates. Six of those graduates were in the Chilean military junta that overthrew the Allende government.[23]

Following the death of Salvadore Allende, democratic Chile, proudly described by Chileans as the "England of the South," was plunged into a military dictatorship that used Nazi-like methods of torture, murder, and repression calculated to bring total control over vast sectors of society.[24] Arbitrary brutality, such as occurred in Calama, a small mining town some one thousand miles from Santiago, became common occurrences as reminders to the people that resistance was useless. In October of 1973, military men arrived in Calama, arrested 26 men, and shot all of them to death. They then went to the houses of those men and told their wives that they must never speak about what happened. If they were to utter a word, their children would be killed.[25]

You are connected to these Women of Calama, as they are called today, as well as to all the victims. Chile's "basic institutional structures, including the state terror system, were put in place and maintained by, or with crucial assistance from, U. S. power."[26] Even after the Pinochet regime murdered Orlando Letelier, Allende's foreign minister, on the streets of Washington, D. C. in 1976, the U. S. government took no effective steps to stop American support for the dictator. At that same time, "U. S. banks lent Chilean institutions more than $1 billion, and major corporations undertook large-scale investment programs."[27] General Augusto Pinochet was the leader of a *client* state, an ally in the Cold War.

What happened in Chile is not a part of the American dialogue or the American consciousness. So consumed are we with managed news without historical perspective, ball scores, and gossip by and about politicians, that the last word concerning Chile might just as well be from former CIA director William Colby. Colby excused the executions carried out by the military junta. In his words, they did "some good" because they reduced the chances that civil war might break out.[28]

Article Four discussions will explore comparisons between Chile and Guatemala, Laos, Cambodia, Nicaragua, Panama, Indonesia, El Salvador, East Timor, and others to the ends of the Earth. *Our own conduct*, I think you will find, has created the enemies we now face. The Ayatollah Khomeini and Saddam Hussein came to power as a result of our forcing on the peoples of Iran and Iraq puppet governments which were out of step with the wishes of their own people.

Peace is won not by force of arms but by peaceful dealings. Earthceding is the very first step. Hasn't the time arrived to use the domestic violence clause of Article IV, Section 4 to help us accept the responsibility of accurate memory and of correcting the ills we've created?

CHAPTER 17

IN THE SPIRIT OF 1787

If, under Article IV, Section 4, the United States is to disarm and do Earthceding, just how will that affect international order and the avoidance of war? I believe that our disarming and Earthceding are the first necessary steps to world peace and security.

While the United States may have "won the Cold War," as our politicians enjoy boasting, we have not come anywhere near accepting responsibilities involved with victory and military control. As John le Carré aptly pointed out, "...the Western powers never had the faintest idea what to do with the world if they ever freed it from Communism."[1] As a result, 100 wars may be raging around the globe at any one time and the United States intervenes only if intervention is thought to be in its own interests. Better said, intervention occurs only when it will benefit the dominant economic groups. And so it is that American troops and weapons were used to protect the oil interests by an invasion of Iraq but were not used to stop years of genocide in Bosnia. World order and world peace can not be served by such a master as the United States. Nor is there another nation which would be master for the benefit of the Earth and its people.

The need for a true world government has never been so manifest. As Bertrand Russell put it: "Science has made unrestricted national sovereignty incompatible with human survival. The only possibilities are now world government or death."[2] Earthceding must include a substantial grant of sovereignty to the United Nations–a United Nations allowed to be different and more effective than now permitted. Recalling Abraham Lincoln's words: "As our case is new, so must we think anew and act anew. We must disenthrall ourselves, and then we shall save our country."[3]

Insecurity from environmental harms is the present danger that overshadows all others. While the risks may take different forms locally, cumulatively they are national and international threats to survival. As a result, all human conduct that respects, conserves, and cleanses the Earth has to be encouraged. All conduct that wastes resources or damages the Earth is to be discouraged. A first principle, therefore, of a newly constituted United Nations ought to be protection of the Earth, its peoples, and all in the environment.

Such a body might, on occasion, find it necessary to actually interfere with the internal affairs of a sovereign nation that is unmindful of its obligations to the Earth. Where governments are controlled by dominant economic interests to the detriment of the environment (as is so frequently the case), action by the United Nations would be mandatory. Who determines when to interfere and what shall be the standards is a daunting task. Far more daunting, however, is a United Nations that doesn't undertake that mission.

In no case can the Security Council, a relic of the Cold War, be maintained. Dominance by the major powers has actually proven to be so environmentally irresponsible that one-nation-one-vote must be the rule. And, where any discrete group or individual within a nation can make an argument that his or her country is about to waste or destroy the environment, that group or person should be able to command a hearing at the newly constituted United Nations. In a real sense, human desires for survival would be heard as never before over the thunder of economic forces—as it must be.

How can we, in our Article Four meetings, be aiming so high? The answer is that we can aim for no less and still be true to the principles as set forth in Article IV, Section 4 of the U. S. Constitution. Every government, from the most local, through the national, and to the international, owes us the obligation of protection to assure survival. That is their core function. While the U. S. Constitution is explicit on the matter, it is inherent and implied in every contract between the governed and the governors, the individual and the various states. We are owed, if nothing else, survival. And, if not accorded that right, what legitimacy has that government which holds other interests higher?

History has been marked by war and dominance. We can no longer afford that paradigm and survive. The world awaits our decision to Earthcede to an international body strong enough to assure an end to war and the marshaling of resources into protection of the Earth and all within it.

How can one hope that the powerless and the powerful can find common ground sufficient to put into practice a world government as above described? Has it happened before that power was so readily given up for the common good? It has, and the place was Philadelphia in 1787. The fulcrum that brought it about was the philosophy embodied in Article IV, Section 4 of the Constitution. Accommodation for the sake of survival was the very spirit of the Convention of 1787.

The framers, representing the equivalent of independent nations, understood that they were at risk from dangers both internal and external. To meet these dangers, they gave up large measures of sovereignty to create a strong central government charged with the responsibility (Art. IV, Sec. 4) to protect them. Our risks are many orders of magnitude greater. As Carl Van Doren urged, "Their undertaking" ought to be considered "a rehearsal for the federal governments of the future." Van Doren summed up the need for a United Nations modeled as previously described: "No difficulty in the way of a world government can match the danger of a world without it."[4]

The people are now in desperate need of Article Four protections by governments. Whether protections for all of us arrive too late for survival may be determined by the attitudes of those who presently hold significant reins of power. As the framers did in 1787, so should the powerful now loosen those reins for the benefit of survival. Time grows short to resolve issues that will determine whether the Earth our children inherit will be inhabitable.

CHAPTER 18

RECLAIMING IMAGINATION

During Article Four discussions, I watch people react strongly against the ideas that we, not the Russians, created the Cold War and that we were and continue to be a ruthless colonial power. They react strongly against the ideas that the world is not necessarily a dangerous place and that we must allow all other nations to have control over their own internal affairs, that we have to give up a good measure of sovereignty to a world government, and actively demilitarize our nation. The vast majority of Americans resist those ideas. Such thoughts run contrary to commonly accepted beliefs. Most Americans believe that the Cold War was thrust upon us by the Russians, that we spread democracy around the world, that we have a right to interfere with the internal affairs of nations we do not like, and that in this "dangerous" world the United Nations is worthless, so we have to be ever more militarily strong.

There are hurdles that must be dealt with in implementing remedial measures under the domestic violence clause of Article IV, Section 4, such as logistical problems, political concerns, and raising sufficient funds to effectively communicate a message. These hurdles are expected in any such effort and are manageable. Getting people to question and to give critical thought to the commonly held beliefs that support our present business centered, national security state is more than a hurdle; it is a barrier. Discussions of the domestic violence clause, however, that do not include vigorous questioning of some of America's basic assumptions will be as futile as sowing seeds on concrete.

The capacity to critically assess our history and our place in the world requires a number of skills and abilities. Among them are imagination, energy, forthrightness, desire, and will. It is by no means easy work. If there is, however, one attribute that is more significant than all others, it is *imagination*. Imagination is the fuel that drives one to conceptualize anew and gives people the courage to create necessary changes in the world.

I believe that resistance to ideas that tend to run counter to commonly held beliefs is an especially high barrier in America because of the harsh treatment meted out to those who chose to use imagination. Imagination itself has been hunted down and punished. Great pains have been taken to exclude it from our lives, both public and private. In short, an Article Four movement is bound to fail unless unusual efforts are made to reclaim our collective imagination.

Some historical perspective is necessary for an understanding of just how thoroughly the propertied and the privileged have warred against the use of imagination by and for the citizens of our country. Indeed, their war has been against freedom of thought itself.

The beginning of the 20th century witnessed a great and sustained burst of imaginative political energy. Corruption and control of government by monied interests had been ongoing since the conclusion of the Civil War. Historian, Claude G. Bowers, referring to that descent into political indecency said: "Never have American public men in responsible positions, directing the destiny of the Nation, been so brutal, hypocritical, and corrupt."[1] Unregulated business monopolies delivered great wealth to the few and visited child labor, low wages, slums, dangerous workplaces, spoiled meats, and decayed foodstuffs on the less fortunate.[2] Reform legislation aimed at ending the abuses was continuously blocked in the United States Senate[3] by a cadre of senators selected by and made wealthy by the corporate interests.[4] Reform came with an unexpected suddenness between the first administration of President Theodore Roosevelt in 1901 and 1917, the time of our entry into World War I during the administration of President Woodrow Wilson.

The Seventeenth Amendment to the United States Constitution, calling for direct election of senators by the people, was ratified in 1913.[5] No longer would the Senate be an obstructionist body, deaf and blind to fervent needs of the people.[6] State legislatures, now free of the bitter, corrupt, and scandalous job of electing U. S. senators,

could begin to function in a manner consistent with public needs.[7]
Wealth was taxed as never before with ratification of the Sixteenth
Amendment in that same year, 1913; it gave Congress the right to
assess and collect taxes on incomes from whatever source derived.
The Roosevelt-Taft-Wilson era between 1901 and 1917 came to be
known as the Progressive Era. During that time, governmental
structures were, at long last, put into place to begin cleaning up politics and to embark on regulating business, transportation, and fi-
nance.[8]

Leaders of the business community were shocked by this
sudden turn of events. Not that they were actively in favor of slums,
bad food, and child labor, but they generally believed that the Progressive Movement interfered with the "natural order" of things. The
conservative thinking of the day was that *business had been or-
dained to be the dominant interest. Government existed to serve
business and exercise control over the people.* According to this
medievalist view, matters such as slums, bad food, and child labor
would work themselves out in time, "naturally." Interference of any
kind would tend to make the problems worse. The conservative who
adhered to that philosophy believed that he or she was not turning
away from the social issues of the day. Rather, it was considered to
be an enlightened philosophy based on a "higher truth" that was not
always appreciated by "the masses."

To the conservative, the Progressive Movement was a bullet
aimed at the heart. Not only would it have put government at the
service of the citizen, it imagined an international order that was to
make wars obsolete. Artists, writers, and reformers were creating
models for peaceful internationalism where none existed before; the
clay with which they worked was the imagination. Nor was progressivism at the turn of the century limited just to the United States.
On the wings of the "Russian Renaissance," an exuberantly creative
cultural period, Tsar Nicholas II championed a permanent international body for resolution of disputes between nations. The Tsar's
imploring letter of 1898 to all governments of the world resulted in
the convening of an 1899 conference in the Netherlands. At the conference, a Russian proposal for freezing armament levels was defeated. The convention (known as The Hague Convention) did agree,

however, on rules of warfare and established a permanent international court of arbitration. Nicholas himself, in 1905, submitted a dispute with England to The Hague, and, in 1914 on the eve of World War I, urged Kaiser Wilhelm II to use his best efforts to see that the dispute between Austria and Serbia also be submitted to The Hague.[9]

Conservatism in the United States dodged the bullet of progressivism with our entry into World War I in 1917.[10] Just being in a state of war tends to move public opinion away from controversy and discussion of social needs that might conflict with a war effort. To this inevitable and temporary condition, however, was added an additional factor of immeasurable proportions; 1917 was the year that a communist party, the Bolsheviks, attained control of the government of Russia. That event proved to be traumatic to the wealthy of American society, who panicked at the thought that the Bolshevik revolution might somehow triumph in America and their shares, their property, and their privileges would be taken away with a suddenness similar to the unstoppable march of the Progressive Movement.[11] *Their reaction of intense and abiding fear was a watershed in American history that set events in motion from which we have yet to recover. Their fear caused them to begin the long war against imagination and worse, against freedom of thought itself.*

The first victims were the Socialists, a small but vocal political party that embraced the Progressive agenda and stood for the proposition that government ought to deliver essential human services instead of depending on the private sector to do so. The socialists spoke out against American involvement in World War I, referring to it as a rich man's war and a poor man's fight. Theirs was not an isolationist view. Rather, they believed that working people in all countries should find ways of avoiding international disputes that could lead to warfare. As a result of their speaking out against the war, the leadership of the American Socialist Party was tried and convicted of offenses under the federal Espionage Act, which was read by the U. S. Department of Justice to make disagreement with official foreign policy a criminal act. The Socialist Party in the United States never recovered from being thus criminalized.[12]

The socialists of that period committed no crimes, as such. They, however, had the misfortune of daring to exercise, as was their right, imagination to envision a peaceful international world order. So thorough was the annihilation of the socialists in America that they never were a factor in presidential elections and there has never been a socialist governor of any state. In all probability, you have never met a socialist or heard a socialist position on any public question. Whether they are right or wrong on any given issue is beside the point. You have been denied a full spectrum of expression on a host of public questions, especially solutions to problems that entail collective citizen action. Socialists have been active participants of the governments of Canada, England, France, and Italy, to name just a few. In the United States, fear ruled, reason fled, and imagination as well as freedom of thought suffered an irreversible blow.

At the end of World War I, the business interests embarked upon an enormous peacetime propaganda campaign, describing Bolshevism as the "new menace." Labor unrest stemming from postwar inflation was falsely characterized in newspapers as a communist grab for power. Bombings that were probably the work of a few deranged individuals were passed off as proof that the Bolsheviks were attempting to take over the country. In 1919, United States Attorney General, A. Mitchell Palmer, began massive illegal deportations of immigrants and created a new General Intelligence Division (GID) within the Department of Justice. By January of 1920, that Division had become the central focus of the Department. It collected information on over 450,000 people believed to be "radicals." The GID raided publishing companies and private libraries to find what it considered to be offending literature. It sent out swarms of informers and agents in such numbers that they would often comprise 75 percent of suspected "radical audiences."[13]

Almost overnight, the propertied and the powerful had transformed a free American people into a cowed and frightened herd. Alfred George Gardiner, a visiting British journalist, in 1919 noted "the feverish condition of the public mind...hag ridden by the specter of Bolshevism...the horrid name 'Radical' covered the most innocent departure from conventional thought." America, according to Gardiner, had become "the land of liberty–liberty to keep in step."[14]

115

There was no threat to America other than the expression of ideas that were displeasing to American business interests. Further, there was no threat from communism abroad. As previously noted in Chapter 15, while Attorney General Palmer was hunting "Reds" in the United States, an international force of fourteen nations, including the United States, had invaded Russia, participating in an effort to unseat the Bolsheviks from power. That Russian expedition started in 1918 and did not conclude until 1921. Even if the Bolsheviks of Russia intended to overthrow the government of the United States by force, they could have taken no steps in that direction during the years of the Palmer hysteria. They had their hands rather full fighting for their existence against an actual foreign invasion. The "red scare" and the "new menace" were simply ways of controlling Americans by engendering fear, calling for patriotism, and limiting imagination. *The Cold War had its origins in 1917.*

Those years of hysteria brought fundamental changes to the American character and American institutions. People learned that speech was anything but free and taught that to their children. Public speech and thought became tailored to fit a chamber of commerce type jargon. Fear of unusual ideas was everywhere, and the difference between communism, socialism, progressivism, and liberalism was much blurred. If you were young at that time and wanted to advance, you were well advised to speak ill of "radicals." The young lawyer at the General Intelligence Division of the U. S. Department of Justice who oversaw the collection of information on more than 450,000 persons suspected of "harboring radical ideas" should have been censured. Instead, he was later elevated to the position of Director of the Federal Bureau of Investigation and would continue the work of hunting for "subversives." His name was J. Edgar Hoover. The business community learned that it could, whenever it felt threatened, spread fear throughout the Republic and count on the government to punish those with opposing opinions. The governmental institution for accomplishing that purpose was, as above noted, put in place at the end of World War I. It is best described as an "extralegal, autonomous, and clandestine...*political police system*" whose purpose it was to muffle dissent in order to "protect the status quo," maintaining only the appearance of actual political democracy.[15] (emphasis added)

Poets and writers are the lifeblood of civilizations. They live to take our language, fill it to overflowing with imagination, and give it back to us as a gift. As expressed in Chapter 6, they tend to be the seers and forecasters for us, as well. The American political police system has been particularly harsh on them. Carl Sandburg was recognized as a poet of the people. The Federal Bureau of Investigation (FBI), for reasons known only to itself, put him under investigation from 1918 to the time of his death in 1967.[16] Extensive surveillance was maintained on Ernest Hemingway, not because he posed any sort of threat to do criminal acts, but because, in the words of an FBI agent: "His views are liberal and that he may be inclined favorably to Communist political philosophies."[17] Ideas, not criminals, were the sworn enemy of the American government. Reading or assigning the novels of Sinclair Lewis to a class for study subjected one to being labeled a "Communist sympathizer."[18] The 1952 McCarran-Walter Act conferred wide discretionary power upon the Attorney General of the United States to deny travel visas to foreigners. That discretion was used to deny permission to speak in this country to world acclaimed writers and thinkers, including Graham Greene, Gabriel Garcia Marquez, Jan Myrdal, Aldous Huxley, and Hannah Arendt.[19] In like manner, Arthur Miller was invited to attend the premiere in Brussels of his play, *The Crucible*, which was considered critical of American anti-subversive hysteria in the 1950s. He was denied a passport because his going abroad was considered "not in the public interest."[20]

The collection of dossiers on people suspected of having radical ideas numbered 450,000 in 1920. By the 1980s, the number of such dossiers kept by the American political police system (FBI, CIA, and several military intelligence agencies) was easily in the millions. One of the most unfortunate uses of that collection of information was its effect on hiring government employees and filling higher echelon appointed positions. The potential employee or appointee had to be "cleared" for "security" purposes. His or her file might contain faulty information, incomplete information, and the individual would probably be judged by federal agents using criteria quite at variance with reality. The applicant was never shown the file or files and had no chance to rebut what they contained or comment on the criteria for judging. As a result, a multitude of people who would have given of themselves to government service were denied that opportunity because of their political beliefs.

An exchange of letters between Archibald MacLeish and J. Edgar Hoover in the early months of 1942, just following the Japanese attack on Pearl Harbor and our entry into World War II, is most revealing.[21] MacLeish, a highly recognized poet, at the time was the Librarian of Congress. Owing to the suddenness of war, he became obliged to hire employees to staff an Office of War Information. He did so, but many qualified applicants were denied security clearances with notations that they were associated with liberal groups, communist groups, or were suspect because they assisted or favored the Spanish Republic in the late 1930s. MacLeish implored Hoover in writing to instruct his investigators that liberalism should not be considered as suspicious. "Liberalism," he wrote, "is not only not a crime but actually the attitude of the president of the United States [Franklin D. Roosevelt] and the greater part of his administration." In addition, he pointed out that being in favor of the Spanish Republic was an effort to help a legitimate government against a fascist revolution supported by the German Nazis. "Wouldn't it be possible," asked MacLeish, "to instruct all investigators that the people we are at war with now are the same people who supported Franco [leader of the fascist revolution] in the Spanish Civil War."

Hoover's written response was a curt statement that his agents do their work with "absolute integrity." What MacLeish wasn't told was that Hoover had a file on him in which MacLeish was designated as too liberal. In 1962, the poet offered to serve in an unpaid post as an advisor on the arts in the Kennedy Administration. The ever vigilant J. Edgar Hoover alerted FBI offices all over the country to dig something up on MacLeish. Of course, no criminality was found. President Kennedy's death ended the advisory committee upon which MacLeish wished to serve.

The exchange of correspondence between MacLeish and Hoover puts a number of things clearly into focus. First and foremost is the fact that even though World War II had just started, the

FBI, and indeed the entire political police structure, was still fighting against the Bolsheviks' victory of 1917. Americans who favored the Spanish Republic were not looked upon with admiration for their early opposition to Nazism. Rather, they were looked upon with mistrust because the Russians, among others, supported the Spanish Republic. Nazism did not strike fear into the hearts of America's monied interests, but communism did. America did not and might never have chosen to oppose Hitler's Germany militarily. We went to war against Germany in December of 1941, more than two years after the war started in Europe, only after the Japanese bombed Pearl Harbor. Because the Japanese and the Germans were allies, we necessarily found ourselves at war against Nazi Germany. MacLeish's reminder of this history did nothing to dissuade Hoover. The American political police structure was busy warring against imagination and freedom of thought and was not to be deterred, even by the wartime conditions that prevailed in 1942.

The exchange also points up how unaccountable was the FBI for its actions. Hoover never felt obligated to answer the questions posed to him. His was the ultimate power of keeping a file for later use against anyone who questioned his operations and his assumptions.

Finally, we all lost the public service that MacLeish and others like him would have delivered had they not been targets of the political police system. We were entitled to their insights, their patriotism, and their unique talents. Frederick L. Schuman was the Woodrow Wilson Professor of Government at Williams College. In 1942, he suggested that we break diplomatic relations with Franco's fascist Spain and urged that we seek peace through a federation of united nations. In 1950, he noted that America and Russia, unlike fascist governments, did not actually require war and conquest in order to avoid collapse. He predicted that the two superpowers would eventually make peace, but not before both made much use of the Cold War for their mutual purposes. For his brilliance and imagination, Professor Schuman earned an FBI file that excluded him from participating in government.[22]

Thousands of imaginative men and women, like Frederick Schuman, spent their careers sidelined by our political police system.

In their place came a steady stream of like-minded cold warriors whose policies went untempered for lack of opposing points of view in high places. As a result, and in your name, from 1946 to the present, the United States has been out of control, wreaking havoc around the world in a desperate and unchecked effort to return the world to a time when the Bolsheviks didn't exist and governments would not even attempt to control business.

Chapter 16 has set out in some detail our successful efforts to destroy democratic self government in Chile. Chile, once considered the England of the South, is now a place where a military government controls the people while businesses and the wealthy international interests operate without interference by government. The clock there has been turned back to pre-Progressive Era circumstances.

There were no imaginative people in high enough places to say that what we were doing in Guatemala was illegal and immoral by every conceivable standard of decency. In 1952, a democratically elected Guatemalan legislature enacted modest programs of tax and land reform that would allow more peasants to own and cultivate their own land. Your CIA reacted by training and directing the movements of an invasion force. The CIA then brought about the bombing of Guatemala City and other important urban areas until the duly elected President Jacobo Arbenz Guzman agreed to leave office. We then engineered the replacement of Arbenz with one Colonel Carlos Castillo Armas, who put an end to land and tax reform to the benefit of the American owned United Fruit Company. Election by secret ballot was ended, and anyone even suspected of leftist leanings was arrested and imprisoned.[23] Guatemala remains to this day a military dictatorship in which the army closely monitors conduct and speech in the academic, religious, and political spheres.[24] Over 110,000 civilians have been murdered by the military, and many of the leaders of that military who organized torture and murder did so while on the CIA payroll.[25]

There were no imaginative people in high enough places to stop the American political police system from gross violations of the principles of democracy in Brazil.[26] Your CIA spent over twenty million dollars in an unsuccessful attempt to defeat the election ef-

120

forts of nationalist, non-communist President João Goulart in 1962. If the ideals of the United States stand for anything in the world, they stand for the right of people to make political determinations affecting their own lives by free elections. On that score, the words of Thomas Jefferson have circled the earth as both a lesson and a promise of moral support. In 1962, however, the new lesson we were teaching was that we would interfere even into the sanctity of elections for the protection of our business interests. Goulart won in 1962, notwithstanding our efforts. We then orchestrated a military coup. The junta that seized power was immediately recognized by the United States as a lawful government (compare Cuba). Democracy was over in Brazil. Gross human rights abuses followed, including the torture of some fifteen thousand political prisoners and genocide of Amazonian aborigines. The natural resources of the Amazon Basin became the property of heedless opportunists, including many American companies and international financial interests.

We were not driven by the Russians or by events beyond our control in Brazil, Guatemala, or any number of such places as we destroyed people and their democratic institutions. Our motive was, and remains, control of the world's resources in the "national interest," equating the national interest with the "interests of ITT or Kennecott or some other corporation" that feels it ought to dominate resources in a weaker nation.[27] In your name, the CIA did such things for the benefit of the major international corporations.[28]

To this day, our foreign policy remains unimaginative in the extreme. Iran provides a fine example. Wishing to be the architect of its own economic destiny, the Iranian parliament voted in 1951 to nationalize the British owned company that dominated its oil production. Iranian Premier Mohammad Mossadegh, an ardent nationalist, opposed all foreign control of Iranian resources, including attempted efforts to obtain oil concessions by the Soviet Union. In 1953, the CIA organized and directed a coup that overthrew Mossadegh and put Iran under the iron control of the Shah Mohammad Reza Pahlavi. For the first time, American companies were permitted to participate in the production of Iranian oil, receiving a forty percent share of the deal.[29] The Shah retained power through the use of a particularly cruel secret police system. He was finally overthrown by a fundamentalist Islamic government that now holds power. If nothing else, the Iranians can lay valid claim to our wrongful involvement in Iran's internal affairs. Rather than to deal realistically with the turmoil and hatred of *our own creation*, rather than to admit error and call for a retracing of steps, our CIA has formulated plans to spend four million dollars in a secret campaign to spread propaganda to the people of Iran denigrating its own Islamic government.[30] Such a campaign does not have the slightest chance of working. Those who control American policy, however, have no need for an effective foreign policy; the rise of Islamic fundamentalism, which we have brought about, has become the new bogeyman around which to build a new foreign policy screen based on militarism. That new falsehood will be used to justify brutalizing peoples around the world in order to control resources that rightfully belong to them. The cold-warriors continue.

The financial interests that created a worldwide war against thought and imagination have been successful beyond their wildest dreams, most of all in the United States itself. Not only has the language of our politics and our leadership been shorn of dynamic qualities, we the people have been made somehow hollow. Not heeding the advice of Britain's chargé d'affaires Frank Roberts in 1946 that we be the epitome of fairness in the world (Chapter 15), America took the low road against the alleged communist threat. In our rage and through fits of destruction, we have killed and been responsible for the deaths of *over six million people*. Vietnam, Cambodia, Laos, Indonesia, East Timor, Guatemala, Brazil, Iran, and Nicaragua are only a few venues of death and torture. Yet, the American people are not capable of processing what we've done. I believe we have been hollowed out by design, and that in order for us to return to spiritual health, we must face what we have done both in the world and to ourselves. If Article Four discussions do that alone, they will have performed brilliant public service. We can not get to the purposeful, collective, public work that the domestic violence clause entails until we heal ourselves emotionally from the havoc that some part of us knows we visited upon the world. Unless we understand that government can be better, we will never trust government again, even though we desperately need what only appropriate government can accomplish.

How did we get so damaged in our collective souls? How did we become so hollowed out? The answers are all within our memory. We, however, fail to connect the self-inflicted traumas with their necessary consequences.

For the business community to have the "permanent war economy" that it wanted following the end of World War II, a climate of fear about communism had to be created at home.[31] Because the wealthy of America so despised the very idea of communism, the public campaign of hate was driven far too vengefully. In the words of historian Richard Hofstadter, our anti-communism became the "Great Inquisition," as the extreme right wing of the country used it as a weapon to turn the clock back to a time before communism, income taxes, and intrusive government.[32]

The CIA, as envisioned by Congress and President Truman in 1947, was to limit its operations exclusively to other nations. Truman had grave fears that if allowed to operate domestically, the CIA would end up being a "Gestapo" in America.[33] Opposition of any sort and for any reason to government policies in the 1950s, however, was viewed as treason and subversive to nation, family, and the social order; it was to be hunted down and up-rooted.[34] Pressed into service within the country by the business interests that so feared loss, the CIA, however, conducted a good share of its activities right here at home. So secure was that organization about performing its extensive but illegal activity on the home front that in 1964 it, in direct derogation of Congressional intent, created a Domestic Operations Division within the CIA to handle the work.[35] In fact, more than 100 million dollars of public monies were made available for CIA clandestine operations within the United States.[36]

Secretly and for the purpose of manipulating public opinion, the CIA insinuated itself into virtually every segment of American life, including civic and cultural organizations, business, labor, and charitable groups, churches, universities, newspapers, book publishers, and artists', lawyers', and teachers' groups.[37] The secret war against freedom of thought and imagination was carried on against

American students as the CIA covertly subsidized the National Student Association for fifteen years.[38] A Senate investigating committee in 1976 found that prior to 1967, "the CIA sponsored, subsidized or produced over 1000 books." The committee noted that "a free society can't work if the government, and especially a secret government security agency, clandestinely publishes books, owns newspapers, and hires professors or clergymen to propagandize the public."[39]

Colleges and universities are supposed to be bastions of free thought. The CIA made secret arrangements to fund individuals and institutes at these schools.[40] This covert government intrusion into academic freedoms once held dear was generally welcomed as a price one paid for benefits received; it was considered "the way things are."[41] Propaganda launched from the very heart of what the public believed to be free and open institutions of higher learning and culture was virtually unanswerable.

Meanwhile, in the public arena, the drumbeat that started in 1917 equating all things evil with communism was picked up with even greater fervor after World War II. President Truman gave credence to the false notion that the "government was riddled with spies" by launching a security investigation of some 6.6 million persons between March of 1947 and December 1952. In fact, not a single case of espionage was uncovered, but the great wave of public hysteria, once set in motion, would not subside.[42] Criminal convictions of communists in the 1950s were overturned by the U. S. Supreme Court, which noted a total absence of illegal conduct proven by the government. One federal court said that despite the fact that the FBI had an opportunity to observe the communists in great detail both in the field and at their "innermost counsels," there was no direct evidence of even a single example of criminal advocacy of the use of force or violence to overthrow the government. People had been simply jailed for their beliefs.[43] Nevertheless, the official drumbeat continued. In 1965, U. S. Attorney General Nicholas Katzenbach charged that growing resistance to the Viet Nam War draft was occurring because the antiwar movement was communist-infiltrated.[44] Pronouncements like that did much to stifle dissent and prolong a war that, according to the then Secretary of Defense, Robert S. McNamara, was "wrong, terribly wrong."[45]

The FBI was undeterred by court rulings that communists had been unfairly convicted for their beliefs. It was "an agency aflame with self-righteousness and a sense of mission."[46] Remember, its job was not to uphold the Constitution or to fight against a real threat to our national and personal security. There was no such threat. The FBI, under J. Edgar Hoover, who had served since the days of Attorney General Palmer in 1919, was simply carrying on the dogged mission begun in 1917. The ever faithful and single-minded Hoover was attempting, on behalf of a new generation of the privileged in America, to turn the clock back to a time when communism did not exist and the purpose of government was to control the people so that business interests would be unfettered–the medievalist, conservative dream of public life as it actually existed in 1900 before the Progressive Era. To do that, the FBI had to destroy imagination and war against freedom of thought itself.

"Saturation surveillance" was the new method of control used beginning in the 1950s. Instead of having field agents testify in courts where an accused could defend himself or herself against a formal charge, information generated by agents was used to subpoena people before Congressional committees where they were ordered to incriminate themselves and others or face losing jobs and reputations.[47] The "crime" that this system of informing was attempting to reach and eradicate involved having certain thoughts or associating with others who had such thoughts. To be guilty in the public mind, you need not have been an actual communist; sympathizing with those people or their thinking was sufficiently damning. This was indeed a war against the freedom to think.

Government agents and informers were used for more sinister purposes, as well. They were directed to undermine the efforts of citizens working peacefully in their own organizations to deal with issues of the time. Thus, an FBI agent, under the Bureau's COINTELPRO (Counter Intelligence Program), would write a false letter to someone within a civic organization to sow seeds of dissension. A particularly effective leader would be scorned or ridiculed by an agent using manufactured information and be thereby denied the possibility of leadership. Agents would often make someone a pariah by putting out false information to convince others that he or she was an FBI agent under cover. COINTELPRO activity included assaults, burglaries, letters to employers, creating tax audits, and manipulating people into the commission of criminal acts.[48] This was patently unlawful conduct by the government, carried out covertly, in an effort to disrupt and discredit lawful political activities in such areas as civil rights and foreign policy analysis.[49]

Following are a few examples of the destructive and unlawful conduct of agents of your government. In 1971, there were two separate socialist organizations operating nationally. One raided the headquarters of the other in Chicago, breaking windows and beating up people. The other filed civil suits and had arrest warrants issued. The first organization initiated legal proceedings to obtain control of the headquarters building. A memo from the FBI officer in charge to Washington enumerated the above facts and ended with the following: "Chicago [office of the FBI] is encouraging all of the above through its informants."[50] In another instance, the FBI embarked upon a six year "no holds barred," "felonious" effort to illegally obtain information on and to discredit and destroy Dr. Martin Luther King, Jr. as a leader. Their purpose, under COINTELPRO, was "to promote a new black leader."[51] In the 1980s, the FBI harassed and intimidated people from more than one hundred American organizations who were attempting to voice concern about foreign policy. They were speaking and acting on behalf of victims of our destructive activities in El Salvador.[52] It is naive to believe that the forces that created such patent illegality by government are no longer operative.

In short, the American political police system has created the "political desert of our time."[53] The American dream of having a government responsive to the needs of citizens has not been realized, as a result of the extraordinary weakness of movements for basic change.[54] Fear engendered in the public by the political police system tampered with the very mental processes by which political change is brought about.[55] Fear caused us to censor ourselves more thoroughly than all of our anti-sedition and repressive laws put together.[56] Albert Einstein noted that the government, through militarization, indoctrination, and intimidation, made us timid and anxious, requiring us to organize in peacetime as though our freedom and our very existence were constantly threatened by powerful enemies.[57]

Author, Norman Mailer, earned the enmity of the FBI with these comments: In the guise of protecting us from communism, the government, using fear, "made cowards of a people who had once been passionate, fearless, and bold." We were not even allowed to make our own assessment about communism. "J. Edgar Hoover," said Mailer in 1960, "has paralyzed the imagination of this country in a way Joseph Stalin never could."[58]

This is where we stand. There presently exists a condition of domestic violence in the country as envisioned by the framers of the Constitution. Such a condition, as they well understood, can only be tackled by the federal government. Emergencies, such as this and wars and invasions, are not occasions for maintaining the sanctity of "states' rights" or for overemphasizing the "separation of powers." Article IV, Section 4 mandates "protection" and gives the job to the "United States." The Constitution refers continually to the states and the three branches of the federal government. It says that Congress shall have the power to declare war, the President shall be Commander-in-Chief, and the courts are to have judicial power. Nowhere, other than Article IV, Section 4, does it mention the "United States" as a body responsible to accomplish a task. Situations such as invasions and conditions of domestic violence are actually archetypal events–emergencies that have always and will always require immediate and sustained communal effort.

Sustained propaganda, however, since 1917, has denigrated the very idea that government can or should become involved in collective action for the benefit of the people. Unless actually desired by the business community for such things as canals, highways, and railroads, public action for the benefit of the people has been continually derided as "communistic" or "radical." As previously noted, those people who included the possibility of collective action by government have been persecuted and their ideas have been banished from the public consciousness. Use of the domestic violence clause will necessarily require collective action on a large, federal scale.

Americans can not even comprehend this as a possibility. Neither of our two major political parties has the capacity to enunciate a large and sustained program of federal direct spending for anything other than a military effort. Article Four discussions will fall on deaf ears unless heroic efforts are made to recapture the imagination we once had that included communal activities on a large scale by government for the benefit of the people.

Right now, the bulk of our public money that can be used to put the domestic violence clause to work is tied up in the maintenance of a military establishment. You, your parents, and your grandparents have been continually told how necessary the military expenditures have been. Indeed, the entire apparatus of government, overt and covert, has been devoted to making us so frightened that we will gladly pay for an expensive military establishment. In fact, our military might has been used chiefly to sustain efforts of international business interests to dominate weaker countries so that their natural resources can be exploited by those business interests. That being the case, it comes as no surprise that the demise of the Union of Soviet Socialist Republics, the U.S.S.R., has not been followed by demilitarization. So much propaganda has gone into hiding the true mission for the use of our military might, that the people have no power to even imagine a world without the military or to imagine an international order based on voluntary compliance with bodies set up and maintained for resolution of disputes. We, as a nation, do not even stand for democracy, self determination, and peaceful resolution of international disputes. Our given job, as citizens, has been to pay for the mercenary forces used by businesses to freely take the resources and labors of peoples around the world. We have, in fact, paid for the military domination of poor countries in which our own manufacturing companies get away with paying slave wages instead of manufacturing those products using American labor.

Article Four meetings have to explore the commonly held myth that we live in a dangerous world and have to maintain "forces sufficient to fight a two-front war anywhere in the world," as the military claims is necessary. So impoverished is the public mind on being able to imagine peace that the only question raised on our present plans to build thirty new attack submarines at a cost of 60 billion dollars is which company shall get the contract.[59]

Article Four discussions are an opportunity to share with others how we have been robbed of imagination and have victimized others around the world. Some will say that we should disregard the past as being potentially divisive. That would be so if the interests that engineered deception were no longer around. Such, however, is not the case. The business interests are mobilized and facile, with sophisticated techniques of social control. How else could you be so willing to pay for thirty new attack submarines when the only conceivable "enemy," the Soviets, who had that class of weapons, have disappeared?

Use of the domestic violence clause to change our priorities from waste and war to human and planetary protection will be possible only if we finally disabuse ourselves of fear-bred, false notions fed to us through unceasing propaganda. We, not the Russians, initiated the Cold War. Our overreaction to the existence of communism in the world caused us to spread misery and death throughout the world. We have destroyed democracies, not heralded them. The planet will continue to be a dangerous place until we acknowledge our own primary role in making it so. We have only to face up to our past with regret and apologies in order to help lead the world into a new era of demilitarization, peace, and dependence on a world government for true justice. We will have to show resolve and bravery to undertake exploration of these ideas. Right now, it is our work upon this Earth.

CHAPTER 19

BUILDING A PUBLIC HEALTH SYSTEM

If our domestic crisis had come in the form of a military assault from some organized group bent on taking over government by force, we would know in a minute how to respond and what to do; but it has not taken that well known form. The present crisis involves a threat to your health and the health of everyone you know. In short, it is a threat to public health. Further, it is unprecedented in its scope and fury. A bubonic plague in the 14th century killed a third of the population in an area extending from Iceland to India.[1] As tragic as that was, the plague did not have the capacity to make the Earth itself uninhabitable and turn its civilizations into brute societies. Our present condition of environmental domestic violence does.

The questions that have to be raised are what institutions do we have to deal with such a threat? Are they capable of handling it? If not, what changes have to be made? Keep in mind that the entire resources of the nation, according to Alexander Hamilton,[2] are to be made available to deal with a condition of domestic violence. In our present circumstances, we would stop building such things as stealth bombers and attack submarines and use the money to reconfigure our institutions and retrain people to do the tasks that will permit survival.

At present, our principal institutions that deal with health are government agencies, insurance companies, and the medical profession. Making changes in any of these three, even when those changes are literally and logically crying out to be made, has been most difficult. Government agencies have been belittled and starved of resources. Insurance companies have become so politically powerful that your elected representatives tend to serve them, not you, as clients. The medical profession resisted change even before it became an industry after World War II.

The shelves of your public library are filled with books that are critical of the performance of those three institutions. Yet, they remain essentially unchanged and deeply flawed. What makes this discussion (in the context of the domestic violence clause of the U. S. Constitution) different from any of those works is, as previously noted, the concept of the availability of resources—financial and human resources—to help bring about the required changes. That concept is hard to imagine. Some symbolic act is necessary to let us know that we can afford to do the things we know to be correct. We can afford to pay for the dislocations when major health institutions are changed substantially. Everyone who wants to do a job in the new health systems will have a job, and they will take enormous pride in that work done toward assuring survival. I suggest the symbolic act that needs to be accomplished is the moving of the center of this new health effort into the Pentagon and moving the present occupants into temporary places for downsizing. The Pentagon was constructed during World War II at great cost. President Roosevelt asked Congress for the necessary appropriation, promising that once the war was over, it would be used as a national archive.[3] The time has come to use the Pentagon as a center of operations for a health and environmental effort that can assure survival. When that job is concluded, the complex can be converted into a national archive for the aesthetic pleasure of a vibrant society.

Keeping in mind that we *do* have resources with which to alter, enhance, or abandon our principal health institutions, a discussion of their effectiveness suddenly becomes more than just wishing for things to go right. We can make them go right. The institution or business of insurance as it relates to health protection is the easiest by far to assess. At present, it is the centerpiece of the delivery of medical care. As a health care institution, it ought to be abandoned. Its present prominence in health is based on assumptions about risk and the public's health status that are no longer true.

Insurance has existed for thousands of years. We know a great deal about how it works and why it works. Modern commentators have reduced the question of whether an activity is generally appropriate for insurance to a list of seven criteria.[4] There must be a large number of insureds, potential losses must be significant enough to the insureds so that they will purchase coverage, and the chance of loss must be calculable. The other four criteria are particularly germane to health insurance. They are:

1. Losses should be determined by definite events.

2. Losses should be accidental in nature.

3. There should be relatively few losses.

4. It must be unlikely that a large number of losses occur at the same time.

An endeavor that fits those four criteria well is shipping. At the risk of oversimplifying a complex topic, losses are definite events as the ship and its cargo either make it to port or are lost. If a ship goes to the bottom of the sea, it was likely to be from an accidental event, one that the crew had no control over. Relatively few ships sink, and therefore the amount of money charged per voyage as a premium can be small. Generally, seas are calm and places of danger can be avoided. As a result, it is unlikely that a large number of losses will occur at any one time and thereby bankrupt the insurer.

How does health care providing fit into those four criteria? The first is that losses should be determined by definite events, not situations over which an insured has any control. Insurance companies have long abided by that rule in health care; adherence has made the conduct of carriers actually harmful to public health. Insurance, in this regard, has been a weight too heavy to bear. You can't get an insurance company to reimburse you until you have become demonstrably ill. Illness and disease are the definite events required by the "insurance mechanism," as it is called, in order to satisfy the criterion of certainty. As a result, there is insufficient opportunity for preventive health care using the funding source of insurance. In fact, the term "health care" in the United States is a misnomer. The insurance mechanism sees to it that our money goes almost exclusively to pay for "after the fact measures," as Dr. Joseph D. Beasley, author of *The Betrayal of Health*,[5] calls expensive, hi-tech medical therapies, leaving little if any resources for inexpensive and timely prevention.

Usually, the closest that insurance carriers get to dealing with the prevention of disease is the advocating of early detection. Early detection is a phase that is all too often far too late for health purposes. Some insurers will, for example, pay for mammograms in an effort to detect breast cancer so that it may then be treated. In fact, by the time a cancerous tumor can be detected by mammogram X-rays, the cancer has most often already spread to other tissues, leaving the insured in a dire position.[6] An early detection insurance program may trigger an expensive treatment regimen, but it does not come anywhere near reducing the factors most likely to be driving up rates of breast cancer in the United States. Those factors include exposures to chemical contaminants and radiation, poor nutrition, and careless lifestyle choices such as cigarette smoking and alcohol consumption.[7] In the absence of effective prevention, the incidence of breast cancer increased twenty-four percent between 1980 and 1986.[8] In 1991, the odds of an American woman contracting that disease was one-in-nine.[9] The odds are continuing to increase.

Perhaps you, as an individual, understand the vast difference between health and the absence of disease. In order to attain and maintain good health, you may seek the advice of health professionals who can teach you how to safely rid your body of damaging metals and toxins, how to get the maximum nutritional benefit from foods, and how best to control stress. Your costs for this type of preventive health care will not be paid for by your insurance carrier because you do not yet have disease. In this way, personal, preventive health care through nutrition, exercise, meditation, herbal remedies, detoxification, etc., are trivialized by the American insurance system. The very modalities that can help to keep you in health are not considered definite enough events. The insurance industry requires illness and disease as bench marks. It is inherent in the very nature of the insurance mechanism.

The other three criteria for determining whether insurance is appropriate for any given activity can be discussed together. They require that losses be accidental in nature, relatively few in number, and unlikely to occur in large numbers at the same time. Health insurance was quite likely to satisfy those criteria for the conditions that existed in this country in the 1920s and 1930s. We had not yet so thoroughly polluted the land, the air, and the waters. Agriculture did not depend on chemicals. Problems relating to health, if they occurred, were more likely than now to be the result of accidents or trauma. Such accidents tended to be few in number and not likely to happen in large numbers at the same time. Those were decades, for example, when no one could recall a child having cancer. Insurance for health care may have been possible then.

In the last decade of the 20th century, the condition of America's health has changed drastically. Dr. Joseph Beasley, author of *The Betrayal of Health*, has devoted himself to analyzing the state of our health and how we got to such a circumstance. Just as a business must know its present position and how it came about, we must understand our present state of health and how that came to be. Dr. Beasley appears to be the honest and independent medical accountant that we need to assess present health circumstances. He makes his living as a practicing physician and not a paid expert. He is also the director of the Bard College Center's Institute of Health Policy and Practice. He has been chairman of the Department of Demography and Human Ecology at Harvard University and dean of the School of Public Health at Tulane University. His book, *The Betrayal of Health*, is mandatory reading, "the product of ten years of research on the interaction of the environment, nutrition, and lifestyle and the effect this interaction has had on our health."[10]

Dr. Beasley recounts how our agriculture, consumer protection, water pollution, air pollution, and hazardous waste laws have been inadequate to keep toxins from affecting us.[11] Our bodies, he says, have no effective barriers to these toxins; they accumulate within us and tax our limited capabilities of ridding ourselves of them.[12] Our soil has been depleted of nutrients, and food production is now accomplished largely with chemical fertilizers and pesticides.[13] Compared to crops of the 1920s and 1930s, our nourishment is being "undermined" by foods that are of "reduced nutrient density."[14]

As a result, the doctor notes, there is a substantial increase in damaging cell mutations now taking place, which is playing a major role in our high cancer rates and larger than ever numbers of chronic health conditions.[15] Children are especially vulnerable to toxic exposures and are getting those exposures in the critical fetal development stages.[16] The resulting mutations are causing an increasing rate of damage to future generations that will take the form of more deaths, physical and mental defects, and predispositions to chronic diseases.[17] According to Dr. Beasley, the combination of an environment we've made toxic and a compromised food supply is bringing about increased learning and behavioral disabilities,[18] increased functional illiteracy,[19] and a "steady rise in violent behavior" by our children.[20] In sum, says Dr. Beasley, "people are becoming allergic to the 20th century."[21]

> The benefits and conveniences of today's technology, medicine, energy production, and agriculture have come at too high a price—birth defects, neurological disorders, cancer, and degenerative ailments. Any inquiry into the biological roots of learning and behavioral disorders of the young, or this era's rapid rise in chronic conditions, cannot ignore this pervasive fact of twentieth-century life.[22]

Such circumstances surely violate the three criteria that caution insurance companies to accept business only where losses are accidental, few in number, and not likely to occur in bunches. Yet there is another reason for the insurance industry to refuse further involvement in health matters, and it has to do with civic responsibility. As long as it chooses to remain a key player in the funding of health care, it must, of necessity, require adherence to the first mentioned criterion, that losses should be determined by definite events. That requirement, peculiar to insurance, will make funding for the prevention of disease by eradicating the causes, i.e., sources of pollution and degradation of soil, impossible. If the insurance industry doggedly maintains its position of preeminence in health care, we will for too long continue to spend a trillion dollars a year on treatment of disease and have too little money left for prevention of what is turning out to be a holocaust of human suffering.

Insurance is more than just an industry, one among many whose goal is to make money. Insurance is part of the way we think, use our resources, and plan for the future. It is at the same time a highly personal purchase and an overwhelmingly political activity. So deeply involved is it with our destiny as a people, those who hold places of authority within that industry ought to confer in the light of their Article IV, Section 4 obligations. I believe it to be a civic responsibility for the insurance industry to withdraw from the health field and to help plan for a transfer and retraining of its work force under the domestic violence clause.

A second principal American institution dealing with health matters is the medical profession. How is it functioning? Is it capable of being helpful in our present crisis of environmental domestic violence? What, if any, changes have to be made? How would one go about making them? The medical profession is far more complicated than the insurance industry in terms of domestic violence planning. I believe that, in its present configuration, medicine can be of little help in combating what we face. Making the necessary changes will be difficult, but that can happen in the short time required with a massive, publicly funded effort. The medical profession has become a prisoner of its own success in dominating and destroying competitors. Out of tune with present conditions, it has to be guided to new ways of fulfilling the healer's role.

Your doctor is most likely a caring, dedicated, and hard working person. He sacrificed a good share of his life to get his degrees in medicine. His training, however, was not in how to advise you to be healthy. Rather, he was trained in how to deal with illness.[23] Generally, you don't go to him unless you are ill, and that way of dealing with health has been a dismal failure. Americans are getting sicker as time goes on.[24] Two of the major reasons, as previously discussed, for the escalation of illness in America are nutritional deficiencies and continuing exposures to toxic materials. As Dr. Joseph Beasley points out, today's physician, with rare exceptions, is trained to deal with neither of those problems.[25] Medical school indoctrinated your physician to primarily prescribe drugs, and to do that without even giving him sufficient training in pharmacology.[26] As a result, he relied almost exclusively on pharmaceutical company supplied information during his education and relies heavily upon company salesmen as he practices and prescribes drugs.[27] America's overuse of pharmaceutical drugs has been both costly and dangerous.[28] Drugs are mainly used to "alleviate symptoms" of diseases rather than "identify and treat causes."[29]

Your doctor has unwittingly become a crucial cog in a pharmaceutical company system to sell drugs "whether or not a medical need for them exists."[30] So thoroughly has your physician been indoctrinated, that when you suggest another approach, he may be unresponsive or even hostile. His own medical society and state board of medical examiners might take away his license to practice medicine if he advocates a system other than one based upon symptom alleviation by pharmaceutical drugs.

In one typical case, the New Jersey Board of Medical Examiners sent out an investigator pretending to be a patient to confirm that a certain medical doctor was practicing homeopathy. The doctor had been doing so, openly and exclusively, for almost ten years, having treated more than 5000 patients. At a hearing before the Board in 1992, the doctor asserted the superiority of homeopathic remedies, which are highly diluted substances used for healing that match the unique qualities of each patient and the unique characteristics of symptoms presented by the patient. The homeopathic examination consisted, he said, of lengthy discussions as to both items, as well as observations of the patient by the homeopathic physician. The doctor noted that the investigator-"patient" said the usual diagnostic procedures and medicines prescribed by other doctors had not helped her. He was, said the investigator-"patient," her last resort. The Board, nevertheless, suspended that doctor's license, saying he had placed his patient at risk by his unwillingness to use the usual diagnostic procedures (gastrointestinal endoscopy and blood tests) "mandated by standard medical practice."[31] It didn't matter to the Board that the usual procedures had not worked. Of no concern was whether homeopathy worked, as it was not in accordance with "standard medical practice."

That phrase, "standard medical practice," has been the means by which medicine has, since the founding of this country, isolated itself from the reality of public health and forced practitioners into following destructive paths. In one of America's first and finest literary and descriptive works, *Letters from an American Farmer*, published in 1782, J. Hector St. John de Crèvecoeur allows us to observe conditions in which Americans lived at the time of the birth of this country. On the island of Nantucket, there was no need for "galenical medicines," a phrase Crèvecoeur used to describe the prevailing system of medicine which was based on increasing or decreasing, by the use of unduly harsh drugs and treatments, one or more of the "humors" (blood, phlegm, bile, and black bile) believed by the physician to be out of balance. Americans living there in the 18th century were people made healthy by good food, exercise, and temperance. They were, according to Crèvecoeur, able to deal effectively with occasional ill health through being "extremely well acquainted with the Indian methods of curing simple diseases."[32] The Nantucket experience was not an isolated circumstance. Crèvecoeur encountered women in Delaware who, "when sick they had learnt of the Indians how to find in their woods the remedies they wanted."[33] He visited Anaquaga, an "Indian town" where he saw:

> ...several white people from different parts of Pennsylvania who had purposely come there to put themselves in the hands and under the care of some Indians who were famous for the medical knowledge. Several were cured while I was there; a woman in particular who had a running ulcer in her breast for 5 years before appeared perfectly cured and the ancient wound entirely healed.[34]

It is quite clear that at the time of the founding of this country, there existed a sophisticated, experience-based, "Indian" healing tradition that was well known to the people, inexpensive, and without harmful aspects. That tradition came from tribes that revered nature and understood the spiritual connection between individuals and the Earth and between spirituality and health. American physicians who espoused the correctness of that aboriginal approach to medicine were known as the "botanical practitioners." It takes no stretch of the imagination to realize that had they been allowed to flourish, the practice of medicine would have been marked by the characteristics of awe, reverence, and openness.

A wise medical establishment would have examined and built upon the aboriginal American traditions for the benefit of the people. The fact that such knowledge came from "Indians" and not "white men" was no barrier to its acceptance; it worked. Americans, as Alexis de Tocqueville observed, consistently looked after "the practical side of things," including the "immediate practical applications of science."[35] Wisdom, however, did not prevail. Leaders of the American medical establishment in the 18th century constructed the edifice of "standard medical practice," not in the benign images of the botanical practitioners, but according to a rigid and authoritarian model that was quite at odds with public health.

Dr. Benjamin Rush, a signer of the Declaration of Independence, was a principal architect of that early American medical model. Lecturing at the University of Pennsylvania between 1769 and 1813 to the bulk of medical graduates in the country, he left a lasting mark on the whole of American medicine. It was a vice, he said, for a physician to have "an undue reliance on the powers of nature in curing disease."[36] The all-knowing physician must not shy away from using "heroic" (large) doses of metallic medicines such as mercury.[37] Bold blood-letting was called for in cases of debility.[38] Rush called for blistering healthy tissue by the application of mustard plasters in order to distract the course of disease in some other part of a patient's body.[39]

The important point is not that the American medical system was built upon errors in treatment. Any system errs. The crucial misstep was the creation of a system that was so oblivious to the observations of public health events as they existed. Benjamin Rush actually observed aboriginal Americans obtaining successful results using botanical medicines. He attributed that success, however, to psychosomatic causes.[40] Yet, in his own clinical practice, he (and his colleagues) refused to see the obvious ill effects that mercury, bleedings, and plasters (mainstays of the "standard medical practice") were having on their patients.

As oblivious as early American medicine was to the observation of public health realities, that was how *certain* it was that it was the sole bearer of medical truth. This *sin of certainty* caused the organized medical authorities to refuse access to medical societies to those who used different methods like botanical medicine and homeopathy. They even had laws passed in various states giving themselves a monopoly on the practice of the healing arts for remuneration.[41] The medical establishment, early in the 20th century, succeeded in destroying homeopathy in America by having its professional schools decertified and unfunded.[42] From 1906 and into the 1960s, official medicine carried on a relentless campaign to eliminate chiropractic, which it labeled an "unscientific cult," by continuing efforts to have its practitioners jailed for practicing medicine without a license. A successful anti-trust lawsuit conducted in the 1980s brought significant relief to chiropractors. As a result of that suit, the American Medical Association had to amend its code of ethics so as to no longer forbid referrals of patients by physicians to chiropractors.[43] The code, under legal duress, may have been amended. Referrals by physicians, however, are rare.

Instead of a health care system marked by the characteristics of awe, reverence, and openness, our present medical system is still marked by pride and hostility to other healing modalities. It still practices the "heroic medicine" of Benjamin Rush. It believes itself to be all-knowing. Patients are generally considered to be interchangeable, mechanical units to be subjected to a barrage of drugs and invasive procedures. Dr. Robert Mendelsohn, in his book, *Confessions of a Medical Heretic*, goes to the heart of how medicine is now practiced in Benjamin Rush's heroic image. Medicine, he says, does not just go too far in giving seldom effective but dangerous pharmaceutical and technological treatments, it *"prides itself on going too far."*[44] (emphasis added) As such, it holds itself and its mechanical processes sacred, not "living things."[45]

The medical profession has to move away from its false sense of certainty. We, as a people, are just beginning to understand the unfathomable complexity of healing. We are beginning to understand, as never before, the spiritual connection between body and mind. How can the medical profession exert leadership in this effort if, with rare exceptions, physicians cling so tenaciously to a limited view of mankind and a limited view of healing. Dr. Anthony Carusone is a chiropractor in Garwood, New Jersey. He spends enormous amounts of time studying all branches of the healing arts, from indigenous herbs to augmenting intuitive capabilities to better serve his patients. His thoughts about the necessity to continually broaden one's horizons are particularly meaningful to all people who deal with the public's health. Dr. Carusone believes that "when a person becomes transfixed with just his own reality, he will confuse that reality with the totality of existence and thereby bar himself from the way that leads to truth."[46] That, I believe, neatly sums up how Benjamin Rush's fixation on metallic medicines blinded him from the truth that botanical practitioners of that day were effective without doing harm. So transfixed are the vast majority of modern practitioners of medicine on unnecessarily harmful pharmaceutical medicines and technological procedures that they are unable to even perceive their own contributions to our present condition of environmental domestic violence. Those medicines and procedures are, largely, a source of harm to the public. They constitute vectors of toxins into the public and barriers to gentler healing modalities and preventative measures that are now required by the people. Change must occur rather quickly.

Retraining of physicians on a massive scale has to be accomplished. The only entity capable of such an effort is the federal government. The domestic violence clause was meant to be the central focus for that effort. Think for a moment just how monumental the task of retraining has to be. As Dr. Joseph Beasley points out, doctors must go from relying on drugs that are all mass produced[47] to relying on an in-depth understanding of the patient's uniqueness.[48] In that regard, Beasley quotes Sir William Osler that it is "more important to know what sort of patient has a disease than to know what sort of disease a patient has."[49] Doctors have to go from knowing almost nothing about nutrition and chemical toxins[50] to being experts. Finally, doctors must go from the narrow thinking of simple cause and effect (one disease one medicine[51] to consider (as one does in higher mathematics) complexities and probabilities. As Dr. Beasley puts it, doctors, instead of dealing with "specific causes" of illness, have to be trained to consider "an entire range of contributing factors" that lead to the development of diseases in a complex array of "factors that vary from individual to individual and situation to situation."[52] "The chronic diseases, in their intransigence," Beasley concludes, "point all too clearly to just how much medicine still has to learn."[53]

The retraining should not be organized by the pharmaceutical interests, nor by the federal Food and Drug Administration, which has essentially been captured by both the pharmaceutical and food processing industries, two of the largest businesses in the nation. Who then should coordinate retraining? Who shall write the course syllabus and lead discussions? Certainly, physicians like Joseph Beasley and Robert Mendelsohn. More important would be those who were trained in other disciplines. Leadership in public health has come from nutritionists, chemists, writers, and a host of individuals who were free from the constraints of official medicine's intransigence. Gary Null, a courageous health advocate and investigative journalist, is the latest in a long line of non-physicians who have hammered at the walls of medicine in an effort to infuse medicine with public health realities. Preceding Gary Null were Carlton Fredericks, Adelle Davis, Gayelord Hauser, and a host of others. We learned about the connection between healing and the mind, not from our doctors, but from editor and author Norman Cousins. We learned about the true healing properties of vitamin C from Linus Pauling, a Nobel Prize winning chemist. Rachel Carson, a biologist, brought news that pollution was affecting our health and threatening the natural world.

The line of talented and committed non-physicians active on behalf of the public health goes back to Sylvester Graham in the 1820s.[54] Graham crusaded against the practice of stripping wheat of nutrients in order to make white bread, a food industry practice that we have only recently begun to address. It was the social reformers of the 19th century, more than the drugs and vaccinations of the medical profession, that dramatically improved public health in the last one hundred years. The reformers accomplished that by focusing on purifying our air, water, and by paying attention to our nutrition.[55] This progress by non-physicians was hardly ever recognized by the medical profession. Indeed, it was treated condescendingly, like some recent fad that holds promise but as yet is beneath the concern of a busy profession engaged in more urgent affairs. Thus, the physician who wrote the forward to Adelle Davis' 1965 bestseller, *Let's Get Well*,[56] categorized the book as a "most important" work about the "newer ideas that have developed recently in the field of nutrition" that have attracted interest "even among some professional men." These professional men, however, are so busy "giving the necessary surgical and medical treatment" to their patients that they have "little time to study" these "newer ideas." Nevertheless, if the reader (designated by the author of the forward as a "layman") believes that he has some "condition," the layman (then designated as a "patient") should, rather than self treat, "first see his doctor and find out his trouble. Then while talking over this problem with the doctor, he *might mention* the things he has gained from reading these methods of getting and keeping well." (emphasis added) Such is typical of the damning faint praise that the medical profession uses when speaking of someone it considers an "amateur." Most often, the "amateur," no matter how significant a contribution he or she makes to the common good, is maligned with the designation of cultist or quack. In fact, no progress can be made at reshaping and retraining the field of medicine to fit the public health imperatives of the domestic violence clause without the continuous infusion of creativity and energy of the very people who have, for too long, been denied places of leadership.

The third principal institution dealing with public health is government. Compared to the insurance and medical industries, its connection with health is *paramount*. Americans have permitted excellence in government only intermittently. We tend to chafe at obligations imposed on us by public entities and readily decry our perceived loss of liberties. The public chorus of voices that presently berates and belittles government includes both Democrats and Republicans, as well as liberals and conservatives. Together, they have torn down certain structures of government, rather than repair them where needed. Confusion and harm will follow, as will the need to rebuild government. In the end, civilization itself requires the guidance, wisdom, and resources that only a decent modicum of government can supply. Nowhere is this clearer than when assessing government's role in health protection.

Government, when operating correctly, *reduces and prevents* incidences of disease. Plato said in his *Republic* that the need for many hospitals and doctors was the earmark of a badly run country.[57] When reform governments during the Progressive Era at the beginning of the 20th century began, finally, to regulate the dangerous conduct of corporations, those governments were reducing and preventing incidences of disease on a massive scale. Industry practices that produced child labor, slums, spoiled meat, decayed foodstuffs, and dangerous workplaces had brought about diseases. Those diseases were curtailed by government carrying out its prime function of regulating against harmful activities.

The existence of widespread disease in a people usually means that government has failed in its duty to protect the people. Asbestos, for example, was allowed to be used indiscriminately in the United States as an insulating material. Dr. Irving Selikoff, director of the Environmental Sciences Laboratory at the Mount Sinai School of Medicine in New York, is recognized as the world's leading expert on diseases related to asbestos. He estimated that of the twenty-one million living American men and women who had been occupationally exposed to asbestos between 1940 and 1980, there would be eight to ten thousand deaths every year from asbestos-related cancer through the year 2005.[58] To put it mildly, those will not be pleasant deaths. Commonly, asbestosis is incurable and irreversible. Scar tissue slowly replaces healthy tissue in the lungs until suffocation gradually occurs. Shortness of breath requires that the sufferer keep bottles of oxygen beside the bed and wherever one travels. Coughing can make a person feel as though he or she were being stuck with a thousand needles.[59]

This public health tragedy of monumental proportions was easily preventable. The dangers of asbestos had long been known. In the first century, the Greek geographer, Strabo, and the Roman naturalist, Pliny the Elder, noted that slaves who wove asbestos into cloth developed a sickness of the lungs. In 1900, a British physician, Dr. H. Montague Murray, found sharp and spiky clumps of asbestos in a post-mortem examination of a thirty-three-year-old man who had worked in an asbestos textile factory for fourteen years and suffered from extreme pulmonary distress. In 1924, British physician, Dr. W. E. Cooke, documented and published the facts of a similar case involving the death of a thirty-three-year-old woman. He gave the disease the name "asbestosis." In 1928 and 1929, the British Home Office studied asbestos textile workers and found that the longer they worked with that material, the more likely they were to experience the disease. In 1918, the United States Bureau of Labor published a report that American asbestos workers were dying early and that some American and Canadian insurance companies would not even issue them life insurance policies because of the "assumed health-injurious conditions" of their work.[60]

Allowing exposure to asbestos is not exceptional or unusual conduct by the American government. Rather, it is a common occurrence that dangerous items are allowed to find their way into the workplace and into the home market. Further, the existence of potential harm from exposures already in the population will often be ignored or minimized by government. Dioxin (2,3,7,8-tetrachlorodibenzodioxin) is an extremely potent chemical that is now found in meat and fish. Much of it comes from emissions of incinerators we now use to burn trash. Dioxin has long been known to depress the functioning of the human immune system at extremely low levels of exposure.[61] Levels as low as 2.5 parts per *trillion* of that chemical in the body fat of monkeys are sufficient to cause birth defects in their offspring.[62] As reported in 1987 by Dr. Arnold Schechter, professor of medicine at the State University of New York at Binghamton, average human breast milk in the United States then contained 7.5 parts per trillion of dioxin.[63] While similar levels of dioxin in mothers' milk had moved the government of Sweden to express "intense concern" over the problem,[64] our government was shamelessly minimizing the risk. EPA officials took the position that the amount of dioxin an infant would acquire from mother's milk was not dangerous because it was not that much higher than the amount already acquired in the mother's uterus. Further, according to EPA assurances, babies probably weren't much affected by dioxin because it would be stored in their fat and thus be kept from reaching organs where it can cause health problems.[65] That statement was pure guesswork for the

purpose of political damage control. We created these most dangerous forms of dioxin in massive quantities only recently and know
very little of their health consequences and even less of their effects
in the uterus and upon children being breast-fed.[66]

Writing in 1960, William Longgood observed that cancers in
infants and children just "a few decades ago...were a medical rarity;
now they are commonplace."[67] The existence of so many vectors of
harm, from pesticides to heavy metals and from the degradation of
our food supply to increases in radiation exposures, all of which are
causing so much suffering and diminution of human potential, can be
laid at the feet of government. Government did not come anywhere
near doing the job of keeping harm so far from us that we would
have little need for hospitals and doctors. Every new, heroic, and
expensive medical procedure that ingenious physicians are required
to devise to save young lives from diseases that should not be occurring is yet another affirmation of the failure of government to protect
us. The very existence of our present condition of domestic violence
is proof of the failure of government.

The dereliction of duty by government has been profound.
Certainly, our elected representatives did not often enough function
with the wisdom and independence that James Madison hoped they
might.[68] As William Greider has pointed out, the privileged placed a
"screen" of distortions in front of us, behind which the two political
parties "learned to work as one" on behalf of the powerful—their
"clients."[69] EPA has arguably brought about the "cleanup" of a few
dozen Superfund sites by requiring waste to be moved from one old
leaking site to a new leaking site. That, according to William San-
jour, an outspoken EPA policy analyst, "solves a political problem
because the government is doing something to give people the im-
pression it is taking action to deal with those wastes. But it is not
removing the health threat."[70] In fact, the much heralded 1980 Superfund program has not even begun to seriously address the public
health threat represented by dumped and buried toxic wastes. A
1988 General Accounting Office study revealed that there might be
as many as 427,000 hazardous waste sites in the United States that
are in need of attention.[71]

The Clean Air Act was passed with much fanfare in 1970. Although it authorized EPA to set national emission standards for hazardous air pollutants and gave that agency wide discretion to limit emissions with an ample margin of safety for human health,[72] the government, for over twenty years, refused to do so. While allowing industry to vent billions of pounds of hazardous gases into the air every year,[73] it devoted its efforts almost exclusively to limiting discharges of a certain few pollutants which would make the skies appear cleaner without necessarily being safer. In that manner, the political problem of appearances was addressed, but the public's health was allowed to suffer.

Government officials and politicians will congratulate themselves on reducing the amount of waste discharged into the oceans and the waterways following implementation of the Clean Water Act of 1972. Little is said of what continues to be legally discharged and the health effects thereof. In 1985, one environmental writer, Leo H. Carney of the *New York Times*, calculated the amount of partially treated but still toxic-laden wastewater that flowed daily from sewage treatment plants and industrial pipelines in an area that extended from New York Harbor to about thirty-five miles south along the New Jersey shore. Carney said that the *daily* ocean pollution load from just this one area was 2.4 billion gallons of wastewater, or an amount "roughly equivalent to the capacities of sixteen of the world's largest supertankers, which can carry 157.5 million gallons each."[74] San Francisco Bay every year takes in the equivalent of a mid-size oil spill, about 500,000 gallons of oil and grease, as a result of urban runoff that the government has no effective program to curb.[75]

There are scores of governmental programs that can be similarly described; they function to give the appearance of effectiveness but are grossly deficient at protecting public health and minimizing disease. Government has allowed our food supply, the water we drink, and the air we breathe to be vectors for toxic exposures rather than blessings from a pure and bountiful Earth.

As illness and disease became rampant, government, in tandem with the medical industry, assured that there would be further chemical exposures in the population by granting a near monopoly status to various harsh chemotherapy type products for dealing with the resulting ill health. Declining health, instead of being recognized as an avoidable government failure, became viewed by powerful investment interests as a market opportunity. Ten million people now work in the health care industry, including 600,000 physicians. Spending for medical care is climbing by 12-15 percent per year and totaled nearly one trillion dollars in 1993. In 1992, Americans spent an amount equal to $3,160 for every man, woman, and child in the nation.[76] As Plato would have understood it, government, in failing to prevent this scourge of disease, created the present need for so many doctors, hospitals, dangerous procedures, and medicines. Now that health care is such an economically powerful supplier of products and services to the home market, government is loathe to interfere. On behalf of politically and economically powerful interests, your representatives extol the virtues of the free enterprise medical system as a screen to cover their own failures to protect your health.

The governmental system presently in place that can be used to protect health and reduce the incidence of disease is little more than a skeleton of what it must be to deal with our present condition of domestic violence. Many towns don't even have a health officer. Health officials at all levels have had insufficient training and resources to deal with environmental matters. There is no effective coordination of activities between inspectors from the Department of Agriculture, Department of Commerce, Food and Drug Administration, and the Environmental Protection Agency. Career governmental employees who deal with environmental and public health issues have insufficient job protection, make far too little money, and have woefully inadequate resources with which to accomplish their work. Further, their work is hopelessly politicized by the management level political appointees who stay a short time and then move on to work in the industries they formerly regulated.

Above all else, that part of the public sector that deals with health is mired in *poverty*. While the bulk of America's public dollars were going to producing weapons of war, pennies were being invested in disease prevention. The last two generations of young people overwhelmingly found their career opportunities paid for as an adjunct of our national security state, the purpose of which is to make the world safe for international investments. I remember the painful procedure in 1981 of hiring for a state agency that dealt with environmental protection. Most times, there was just enough money to hire one person. Yet, there were hundreds of resumes from young graduates who geared their educations and their minds to the performance of public service. All but one would be turned away, and that one hiree would settle for half the pay he or she could have received in the private sector. The hiree would then be inducted into a system that was without the resources to come anywhere near doing the job that had to be done. The inability of government to function effectively in health protection was thus institutionalized by a poverty of resources with which to do the job. The public money went elsewhere. Blame for the consequences of badly run programs would fall upon the staff of public agencies. Politicians know how to distance themselves from the government they created. Accepting criticism gracefully and quietly listening to the frustrations expressed by the people were two of the hardest lessons the new hiree had to learn.

If the institution of government is thus so marred, by what magic can it be changed and made effective? Is the domestic violence clause a wand that can be waved to make all glorious things occur? Of course not. The domestic violence clause is, however, the means by which a great mobilization of the people can occur. The gridlock from which we suffer is not government grown too large, but large government listening to and in the service of the few. Government presently suffers from too little democracy and too much reliance on elected representatives who fail to keep in mind the best interests of the public at large.

What will transform government into the instrument it must be is the participation of large numbers of us who are committed to understanding and learning, who have turned away from the many diversions, who have gotten to know truths in the silence, who are reaching for optimum health, and who are strong enough to face the wreckage of a nation thrown into an obvious condition of Constitutional domestic violence. The competent political structure that only we are capable of putting together need be only a short time from fruition if we will put our hearts into the effort.

We have been carefully manipulated since 1946 to believe that we lived in a hostile world. The military structure that we paid dearly for was used then and is used now, not for defense, but to assure cheap and continuing access to foreign natural resources and labor. The companies that benefited from the alleged military threat that we paid for, now, using that cheap and oppressed labor, manufacture their goods in other countries for us to buy. Look around your house and in your closets. Less and less of what you own was made here. Nor were the people of the third world who made our goods paid anything near a living wage.[77] Even with the Cold War over, we are forced by the present political structure to continue supporting a standing army because the purpose of the military was never defense; it was always and remains the control of foreign resources and labor. We are paying for an international empire of economic interests that uses and abuses both the resources of the planet and its people. All the while, we were not told the extent to which exposures to toxic materials at home were making us and our children ill. The public resources that could have been used for disease prevention were, instead, used for "fighting communism,"–a screen to hide the true nature of events. If at any time you or I understood what was occurring and attempted to speak out, our government hounded us and persecuted us in ways reminiscent of the Salem witch trials. And now we are on the edge of a self created environmental holocaust of unimaginable proportions.

The question is: when do we finally respond to build a true public health system that prevents illness and behavioral decline? Is there any fight left in us? For all practical purposes, the health protection mechanisms within government are useless skeletons without our involvement. They are, nevertheless, in place and ready to be infused with purpose. The domestic violence clause is the tool that the framers created for us to use in this crisis. Pick it up. Let's get to work. Let it be said that we did what we were called upon to do.

CHAPTER 20

FOR LIBERALS AND CONSERVATIVES

The gathering of people in large numbers for the purpose of discussing and implementing environmental action under the domestic violence clause will be considered highly political activity. One of the first questions Americans are likely to ask is whether that activity falls within liberal or conservative thinking. We are such a highly polarized political society that you will find the answer to be surprising. Calling upon the federal government to protect us under the domestic violence clause is equally consistent with both conservative and liberal philosophies. Better said, conservatives and liberals need one another in order to properly implement the domestic violence clause. Article Four is the call that brings long feuding siblings home together.

America's liberals and conservatives arose, it must be said, from a common European heritage. Both struggled against the combined power of monarchies and the Catholic Church, which together constituted the Holy Roman Empire. The tie that bound conservatives and liberals together was a fierce desire for political and religious freedom. That desire for freedom of the individual from domination by the state and from the pulpit is no less a shared value today. For all their seeming differences, which one would accept life under a king or be involuntarily bound to a religious order?

The best way to consider the differences between conservatives and liberals is to picture two siblings or business partners or a married couple who aim to make a success of things. One of the two is slow to act, thoughtful, and wants to build upon what has already been successful for them. The other is intuitive and willing to act quickly, even though such action would take the family or business into new ventures. Just about all of our families and businesses contain these two basic personality types. Both care very deeply about the future. Their underlying natures, however, require them to address problems differently.

In political terms, the liberal is likely to seek a "relaxation of the tight hold of custom, law, and authority," ascribing to a "belief that man can control his fate and build a better world."[1] Less trusting in the proclivities of men, conservatives have a "preference for institutions and practices that have evolved historically and that are thus manifestations of continuity and stability."[2]

For example, in 1789, the preeminent conservative, Edmund Burke, foresaw the bloodshed and tyranny that were to follow the French Revolution. He considered that revolution ill-advised because it sought destruction rather than improvement of existing societal traditions and institutions.[3] The American Revolution, on the other hand, was well within conservative parameters. According to Burke, colonial Americans had a long and successful experience with self-government in the English tradition.[4] The American Revolution was not, therefore, a mere destructive upheaval, but an effort to restore colonial prerogatives wrongly taken away by Britain.[5]

Saving, conserving, restoring, and improving upon were consistent themes of Edmund Burke. Biographer, Stanley Ayling, notes that this "constant resort to fundamentals" tends to keep Burke relevant to the problems of succeeding ages.[6] Nowhere is this clearer than in Burke's response to Rousseau's 1762 formulation of the concept of the "social contract," an agreement among the living to attain the mutual benefits of self government. "Society is indeed a contract," conceded Burke, however, it is "not only between those who are living, but between those who are living, those who are dead, and *those who are to be born*."[7] (emphasis added)

In the 20th century, a group with a political philosophy that includes a deeply felt civic obligation of an ongoing contract between the present, the past, and *the future* must necessarily undertake leadership in the environmental field. Conservatism has for too long allowed the environment to be an exclusive territory of liberals,[8] while attempting to hold back governmental efforts in that area with a laissez-faire agenda.[9] There won't be a healthful future for the Earth or for generations to come unless and until conservatives take the words of Edmund Burke to heart, end the obstructionism, and get to work.

Gordon K. Durnil, in his book *The Making of a Conservative Environmentalist*,[10] states the case with great power and authority. He traces his ancestors back to England in the year 1201 when one of them, most probably a conservative, was appointed Sheriff of London.[11] His family began to settle in Indiana in the late 1700s and were involved in the formation of that state.[12] He describes himself as a Republican who has long practiced a conservative philosophy.[13] Convinced that "current environmental policies are putting our children in harm's way,"[14] Durnil calls for conservatives to act: "The time for toxic tolerance is past. It is time for us conservatives to sign on. We can be leaders who make a major difference for our nation, our continent, our globe...we should be leading this parade!"[15]

When Gordon Durnil was appointed by President George Bush in 1989 to be a commissioner on the International Joint Commission, a group that studies and makes recommendations about ecological health of the Great Lakes Region,[16] he was skeptical about claims of environmentalists concerning the existence of threats to public health from toxic exposures.[17] After carefully examining the evidence, he now concludes that "persistent toxic substances" in the environment are probably interfering with human development, beginning at the embryonic stage.[18] In addition to being the cause of increases in diseases like cancer, there is more than enough evidence, he says, to conclude that toxins are bringing on neurological problems, learning deficiencies, behavioral abnormalities, reproductive failures, and suppression of immune systems.[19]

Durnil's book is meant by the author to be the sounding of an alarm[20] to consider true causes for the dangerous world that we have created. Instead of blaming educators, liberals, and bussing for the failure of students to adequately perform in school and in the workplace, he asks: "What if our children are not learning to the extent that they should be learning because some of the persistent toxic substances we have discharged into the environment have di-

minished their ability to learn?"[21] Has our whole population become
dull for that very same reason, he asks.[22] Conservatives who "preach
out" against the decline in learning, the increase in crime, disrespect
by young people, and what appears to be an increase in homosexual-
ity should, according to Durnil, consider the substantial evidence that
these behaviors are caused or augmented by toxins that we have put
into the environment.[23] Why are "we conservatives" more concerned
with children bearing children than with the causes of childhood cancer, he asks.[24] In a magnificent plea that should be heard by all, the
author boldly asks this question: If conservatives believe in individual rights, shouldn't the "insidious invasion of our bodies by harmful
unsolicited chemicals" be considered "the most flagrant violation of
our individual rights?"[25] The "future of the world is in the hands of
people willing to take a stand" on these matters.[26] Gordon K.
Durnil's book, *The Making of a Conservative Environmentalist*,
performs an excellent public service; it can help bring conservatives
together with liberals to make survival possible.

Use of the domestic violence clause to meet the present
emergency brought about by our environmental shortsightedness is
not a thoughtless upheaval of existing traditions and institutions.
That clause was meant for such emergencies and it was the central
focus of a Constitution, which, as written in 1787, was a conservative's document. Evidence that it was a conservative document can
be seen from the fact that, as it emerged from the Convention, the
Constitution contained no bill of rights. (The first ten amendments
were enacted several years later.) Additionally, the only governmental officials the people (white men of property only) directly voted for
were members of the House of Representatives. The Senate could
effectively veto any proposals by the House and had sole power to
impeach federal officials, ratify treaties, and confirm Presidential
appointments to the Supreme Court. Aside from emergencies, the
power of the federal government was meant to be limited. Thus, the
framers created a Constitution very much in the conservative image;
it protected Americans from both the power of the federal government and the potential tyranny of a majority of the voters.[27] Using
the domestic violence clause, a procedure required by a conserva-
tively crafted Constitution, the way is clear for conservatives to join

with liberals to more surely put human and financial resources into safeguarding survival.

The present political schism between liberals and conservatives is forced and unnatural. Human endeavors generally bring together a fair mixture of people of different backgrounds and natures. Within any classroom, boardroom, union hall, or public meeting, there will usually be a good range of people from the too reticent to the foolhardy, with most folks fitting somewhere between extremes. The group then shares opinions. In fact, most of us have a liberal and a conservative bent within us. As discussion continues, we often find ourselves in turn agreeing with extremely divergent views on the same matter. The important point is that the group and each member have the benefit of the interchange of opinions of its members. The divergence informs us and is crucial to sound decision making.

Few human endeavors are likely to be fruitful without deferential inclusion of highly divergent views. One of the better known examples of deference as it should be practiced occurred in Roman occupied Palestine in the early days of Herod's rule. Two distinct schools of biblical interpretation arose within the traditionally accepted framework of Judaism.[28] Hillel, liberal and the founder of one, advocated the use of flexible interpretations of Jewish law that would take into account the intention of the parties being judged.[29] Shammai, conservative and founder of the other school, advocated stringent and uncompromising objective standards for judging all matters.[30] The controversy raged for over a century and was respectfully resolved by the rabbis in favor of Hillel in a decision that included the following famous line: "Both are the words of the living God, and the decision is in accordance with the House of Hillel." That language, according to Talmudic scholar, Adin Steinsaltz, was meant to be an affirmation of the principle that giving preference to one method "does not mean that the other is based on a misconception."[31]

In today's noisy public debates, no room whatsoever is left for crediting the opposing side with a position even worthy of consideration. God may weep for *both* mother and fetus in the abortion controversy, but few participants do. Some commit and condone the murder of physicians who perform abortions, taking the ultimate revenge against people who hold a contrary view. Politics has become a blood sport as opponents are vilified, dissent within the ranks is not permitted, and issues are framed as much to confound as to educate the public. In the end, liberals have given up on the possibility of planning for and boldly creating a better government that would serve the people. Conservatives have mired themselves and the country in a ceaseless blaming of both government and liberals for every evil that they say is upon us. And, above all, public life is mean-spirited. Former New Jersey Republican governor, Thomas Kean, said it well in August of 1995 when he refused to run for the United States Senate. He refused to run because he knew that as a moderate, his party would "marginalize him, put him on the wrong committees, and stop him from getting things done." It would, he said, "be six years of frustration." Further, said Kean: "People are angry at one another and use language aimed at destroying one another. It's so mean spirited down there [Washington, D.C.] that it makes it difficult to sit down and find compromises to get things done for the public, to bring people together."[32]

Only recently have I begun to understand how easily a large segment of the American people became poisoned with hate for liberals. I knew a woman who lived for some eighty years without ever uttering a harsh word for anyone in this world. She made it a point never to indulge in gossip and dissuaded others from its use. In her last year, illness kept her at home, and she listened to the radio for company. One evening, I asked her what she had done that day. She replied that she listened to a particular radio personality, as she did every day. I recognized the name, one of a number of conservative talk show hosts who spend hours every day continually berating liberals.

"You really enjoy him," I said, in the matter-of-fact way which people use when wishing just to keep a conversation going. I shall never forget her response. It showed so clearly how well the pitching of relentless hate will work on even the best of us.

"Yes, I love him," she said, and with a right fist clenched: "And, boy he gives it to *those damn liberals*."

As we continue to pour toxins into the environment and produce food of insufficient nutrient density,[33] public health and human potential will continue to decline. The resulting impairment of the ability to maintain higher order thinking skills brings the brute society on at an ever increasing pace. Historian, Barbara Tuchman's 1987 observation that "the knowledge of a difference between right and wrong is absent from our society, as if it had floated away on a shadowy night after the last World War,"[34] aptly describes our descent into madness. An inability to appreciate the difference between right and wrong is the test for insanity. The present litany of conservative preaching is a heaping of blame upon liberals for causing the decline of family, education, morals, initiative, discipline, and the capacity to work. All of these declines are, in large part, being driven, not by liberals, but by environmental exposures to toxins and a thoroughly compromised food supply.

The behavioral declines will continue as long as public focus is directed to the wrong cause. They will, therefore, be fine fodder for ongoing, long-term Republican demagoguery. That steady outpouring of demagoguery, if not stopped, will act as an anchor impeding all progress in resolving the environmental causes of our declines. I repeat the entreaties of Gordon Durnil for conservatives to undertake responsibilities for the preservation of this Earth and the health and sanity of those yet to be born. I repeat the words of General George Washington in his last wartime circular: "...with our fate will the destiny of unborn millions be involved."[35]

Just as effective and timely use of the domestic violence clause will require the thinking of both conservatives and liberals, they desperately need the public discipline that the domestic violence clause offers. Both need to be yoked together so that they might pull in the same direction, able finally to focus all energies on survival. As never before, this Earth and the generations to follow need the positive energies of us all.

CHAPTER 21

ARTICLE FOUR MEETINGS

Article Four meetings can create the structure for a people's movement that will ensure survival. The fate of the Earth, of our children, and of the unborn may just depend on what happens at those meetings. Great attention, therefore, should be paid to how they are conducted. Above all else, the goal is a search for truth. We, the American people, have lived so long in the shadows of delusion and denial that only the unalloyed truth can get us out of the mess we've created for ourselves.

Assuring that meetings will be purposeful endeavors directed toward wisdom is no easy task. It would be folly to overlook the fact that we have all become, to one degree or another, impaired intellectually and neurologically as a result of a lifetime of exposure to toxins. As a result, we tend to recoil from pursuing the hard work of sorting out troubling complexities in human affairs. Instead, we tend to opt for surface solutions based on philosophies that might easily fit on bumper-stickers. Easy solutions are the palliatives that we embrace in a manner similar to the way Dr. Nation's rats, stressed by toxins, turn to drinking alcohol. Impairment, together with nutritional deficits and a steady diet of mind numbing television and radio, continuous commercial messages, vacuous political campaigns, government propaganda, as well as endless diversions have combined to make us significantly diminished in terms of higher order thinking skills. Despite our outward appearances of confidence and competence, the vast majority of us actually now lack the necessary skills to sort through complexities to reach defining truths.

The importance of facing up to our present condition of human impairment can not be overemphasized. We are not, by nature, inept and incapable of dealing successfully with civic affairs. Nor are we evil or selfish despoilers. I believe that humans are potentially limitless spiritual beings, fully capable of caring for the Earth and for each other. We have, as the noted author Theodore Roszak has said, already begun the process of developing a "significant new sensibil-ity." Roszak envisions a "transformation of human personality in progress which is of *evolutionary* proportions, a shift of conscious-ness fully as epoch-making as the appearance of speech or of the tool-making talents in our cultural repertory."[1] Proof that the shift has already begun, according to the author, is our "new ecological awareness, together with its sense of allegiance to the planet as a whole."[2] We will not, however, come anywhere near reaching our greater, global potential if we fail, in our meetings, to help one an-other rid ourselves of the toxins–burdens we were never meant to bear. The search for truth must include helping each other rid our-selves of those shackles.

Article Four meetings will be places where people will learn how to detoxify their bodies. For generations, government has al-lowed constant exposures through the air, water, food, and has permitted innumerable harmful products into the home market. Fi-nally, there will be an extensive ongoing program at these meetings to embark on the improvement of public health and the prevention of future harm. We will care for one another and teach each other the ways of composting, organic farming and gardening, how to rid our-selves of and avoid harmful chemicals, and how to grow strong with natural remedies and healing modalities. Meetings will be places where we will, together, reach for optimal health on our way to unique public service. The two go hand in hand. "The health of the people," wrote British Prime Minister Benjamin Disraeli, "is really the foundation upon which all their happiness and all their powers as a state depend."[3]

As always, quotes of a different era must be adjusted to fit our present circumstances. Disraeli lived in a simpler time. His views of the goals of public service were appropriate for the middle of the 19th century. To him, good health allowed for service to one's country, the end of all duty. Our views of the world are quickly ex-panding. Not that our country is unimportant, but as Theodore Roszak has pointed out, our consciousness is now attempting to extend beyond the narrow boundaries of nationalism to embrace an allegiance to the planet and all its people. Disraeli's comment transposed into our consciousness for our present needs stands for the proposition that public health is even more a precious commodity than ever before. It is a foundation for both our happiness and human survival on an inhabitable Earth.

In this manner, health, survival, and an expanding consciousness are bound up together. Certainly, anything that degrades consciousness diminishes the possibilities of health and survival. Consciousness, of course, includes higher order thinking skills like logic and calculation. But it is much more. It is the power to be intuitive and to roam freely on wings of imagination. Ultimately, an expanded consciousness permits us to glimpse, perhaps just briefly, at all things sacred. That brush with the eternal is all we need to feel a great empathy for our fellow creatures on this Earth, and it is all we need to direct us to work for survival.

The meeting agendas will have to be as broad as our ways of harming ourselves and each other have been extensive. That litany should include such things as the mercury fillings we've put in our teeth[4] and the damage done by the partial hydrogenation of the oils used in our foods.[5] You will want to study what neuroscientists call "excitotoxins." They are taste enhancing chemicals that the government has allowed to be put into our food. They have the clear capacity to reduce consciousness and human potential. Dr. Russell L. Blaylock, author of *Excitotoxins: The Taste That Kills*,[6] explains how a class of chemicals that we ingest has come to be called excitotoxins. When neurons (the cells that comprise our nervous system) are exposed to those chemicals, they can become very excited, reach extreme exhaustion, and then suddenly die, "as if the cells were excited to death."[7] Dr. Blaylock, a neurosurgeon in private practice in Jackson, Mississippi, wrote the book because he believes that the dangers, especially to small children and older persons, are extremely significant and should not be withheld from the public.[8]

Blaylock points out research that has shown that excitotoxins can destroy neurons in the hypothalamus of the human brain. Damage to that brain structure has the capacity to skew normal growth patterns, bring about an early onset of puberty, and affect "consciousness itself."[9] At the time of initial exposure to these toxins, damage done to children produces no outward effects. In later stages of development, like adolescence, the damage can manifest itself as an endocrine deficiency, a learning disorder such as autism, attention deficit, dyslexia, or an emotional control disorder, including violent episodes, schizophrenia, and paranoia. "Hundreds of millions of infants and young children," says Blaylock, "are at great risk and their parents are not even aware of it."[10]

What are some of the names of these excitotoxins? Cysteic acid, glutamate, and aspartame. They reach us in products containing what is called "hydrolyzed vegetable protein," MSG (monosodium glutamate), and NutraSweet®.[11] Hydrolyzed vegetable protein and MSG have been used widely, even in baby foods.[12] The use of MSG by the American food industry began in the late 1940s and has doubled every ten years since then.[13] Our "dramatic increase" in the use of NutraSweet® moved Dr. H. J. Roberts, an internist practicing in West Palm Beach, Florida, to write his book, *Aspartame (NutraSweet®) Is It Safe?*[14] In it, he says it is "imperative" that researchers who are independent of the food industry study the potential connection between a host of physical and emotional problems, including "brain tumors, Alzheimer's disease, birth defects, seizures, impaired intelligence and behavioral abnormalities among the children of women who ingested aspartame products at conception and during pregnancy."[15] Indeed, Dr. Roberts believes that every person experiencing unexplained "emotional problems" should be asked about aspartame consumption.[16] Government labeling laws are grossly insufficient.[17]

Government will not fight to protect the precious consciousness of you and your family. As the engines of harm like excitotoxins, growth hormones in the meat and dairy supply, lead, cadmium, and PCBs take their awful toll on our children, government is unable to develop a public health strategy to even begin to assess the harm and focus on the multitude of causes. Our youngsters are plagued as never before by violence, learning disabilities, attention deficit disorder, and the angst of being unknowingly poisoned. I believe that they intuitively mourn for the loss of youthful faculties such as joy, ease, gracefulness, and a boundless mental acuity. Instead, government allows and gives its tacit approval to the drugging of the children. The prescription drug methylphenidate, known by its trade name, Ritalin, was, in 1995, being dispensed for the treatment of attention deficit disorder to more than two million children and teen-agers–four times as many as in 1990. Ritalin has much the same effects on youngsters as amphetamines; it is not unlikely that children are becoming dependent upon it. When the drug wears off, the child can experience agitation, tension, and anxiety, the very things, according to John Merrow, producer of a television documentary on attention deficit disorder, that the drug is supposed to correct.[18] Government thus refuses to stop the constant exposures to such things as excitotoxins, which cause untoward symptoms, while it allows yet another toxin, a prescription drug, into the home market, only exacerbating the problem. Heedless of public health, government hardly considers why children are suffering from such things as attention deficit disorder in the first place. What small claim, if any, can we make to being decent human beings if we allow the continuation of a government structure that is so callous?

At Article Four meetings, I will stand up and say such things. I need no official, government approved studies to conclude that the myriad of toxins that have potential to harm are in fact harming my children and yours. Science is more than the studies its practitioners extol; science is, above all else, observation, common sense, and a trusting in our innate sense of appropriateness. Groucho Marx did a comedy scene that epitomizes the way we have been dismissed as observers of the holocaust of harm that we have done and are doing to ourselves. Marx, in bed with his neighbor's wife, shouts at her husband, who has just barged through the bedroom door, that he is elsewhere: "Are you going to believe me or are you going to believe your lying eyes?" I will no longer be so easily dismissed.

Nor will the great majority of Americans of all backgrounds and beliefs be so easily dismissed. The American government, as it is now constituted, has let us all down in the most profound way. We, the people, declared our independence in 1776, saying that no government acts appropriately that fails to respect our self-evident, unalienable, and God-given rights to life, liberty, and the pursuit of happiness. Ill health, declining consciousness, and impaired human potential on the way toward a brute society makes a mockery of our rights to the basic freedoms.

Gary Wills, writing in the *New York Review of Books*,[19] made the outstanding observation that belief that government has strayed from the promises contained in the Declaration of Independence is becoming commonplace. Wills says: "The suspicion that government has become the enemy of freedom, not its protector, crosses ideological lines.... It is no longer so 'extreme' to believe that our government is the greatest enemy to freedom." In his article, "The New Revolutionaries," Wills recalls that liberals were alone in their distrust of government as the CIA, for example, attempted to destroy the life and work of Dr. Martin Luther King, Jr. Since then, says Wills, people who call themselves conservatives have experienced such things as their being used as guinea pigs in nuclear testing by the Defense Department. The Bureau of Alcohol, Tobacco, and Firearms has shown that it can slaughter innocents with the same lack of concern as any out-of-control Russian KGB group. Wills says, and I agree, that the expensive standing army we have deliberately maintained (contrary to the wishes of our founding fathers) has sapped our capacity to create a government structure that is in touch with reality. Our government is no longer entitled to the assumption of legitimacy as it now operates almost exclusively on behalf of the powerful. It will do great harm to us merely in order to maintain control over us.

Seeing this, the "new revolutionaries" ("rightists") organize in ways that the Black Panthers and the MOVE activists ("leftists") could not accomplish. Gary Wills points out how they (the "rightists") openly resist paying taxes. They attempt to bring control over the legal system by encouraging jurors to disregard laws that are considered to be unfair. They want to keep guns and assault weapons (and they organize politically for that purpose) because they have been given reason to believe that the government of the United States has become untrustworthy. And I agree that the government has become unworthy of our trust. The government of the United States has become big and expensive, not in the service of the people, but in the service of the privileged, many of whom received and continue to receive wartime profits during a fifty year period that might have been America's golden age.

I believe that Article Four meetings must be places for the new revolutionaries to contribute their insights and their zeal. Liberals can not and do not defend all aspects of this American government, which is so bent on a standing army and so opposed to the need for public health initiatives. Conservatives who have supported militias and powerful forces fighting for fundamental values understand: (as Wills so well paraphrases their position) "The authority of government can no longer be assumed. It has to be justified from the ground up." Continuation of government on its present course, without challenge, will assure our plunge toward a brute society on a degraded and uninhabitable planet.

That brings us to another polestar rule that Article Four meetings must maintain. The first was to recognize and deal with our impairment. The second has to do with communication. The new revolutionaries will be sitting side by side with the old revolutionaries, activists going back to the 1960s. Victims of a failed public health system will be there too, as well as people who recognize our global environmental responsibilities. How will we all communicate? How can we begin to trust in and understand one another when our major political parties continually fuel themselves on creating enmity between us? The polestar rule that I propose is that we require of ourselves the iron discipline of *listening*. Just as clarity of purpose comes from the silence, the power of connecting, truly being as one with fellow human beings, comes from listening to others.

Listening well is not as easy as it sounds. Yet, once a few simple rules are put into practice, good listening is so pleasurable that people can't imagine going back to the old way. First and foremost, suspend judgment about what is being said until you have actually heard and understood the entire message. Next, assume with as much fervency as you are capable that the speaker is even more well intentioned than you. Then try to imagine yourself living through the experiences that have moved the speaker. Any questions that follow should be solely for the purpose of better understanding what has been said. This is the iron discipline of listening. Excluded from that process is confrontation, accusations, and the telling of a different story or point of view. The people of this great nation do not suffer from irreconcilable differences. We suffer from not hearing one another with clarity and with compassion. As we draw closer to the abyss of life that no longer bears the stamp of true humanness on an uninhabitable planet, we must begin to realize that we are in fact listening for our very lives.

In this manner, the seemingly diverse people gathered together at Article Four meetings can come to understand the commonality of their views. Government, when it undertakes no higher mission than to maintain itself in power, destroys indiscriminately. Those of us who carry in our hearts the killing of Randall Weaver's wife and son, the shooting of students at Kent State University, the unnecessary bloodshed at David Koresh's Branch Davidian premises, and the murder of MOVE activists and Black Panthers are all telling the same story. We all understand that government has to be reshaped into a more humane form and be given challenges befitting our present dire environmental circumstances.

I recently was explaining to an office holding politician my reservations about our government's policy of creating an economic blockade against Cuba. It was causing, I said, so much needless suffering, especially where it involved hunger of children. His reply was chilling: "Why should I care?" It was clear that being enmeshed in the structure of the Democratic and Republican parties was no place to learn compassion. Article Four meetings will be better designed to facilitate listening to people who understand how and why the United States favors the brutal and murdering dictator of Indonesia and, at the same time, works to bring about the downfall of Cuba's Fidel Castro.[20] The meetings will explore how and why we could so casually bomb and destroy lives and properties of the poor in Panama while pursuing the capture of Manuel Noriega, the one-time leader of that country.

To use that fellow's phrase, "why should we care" about murder and mayhem and suffering that we have created throughout the world? Why is that germane to Article Four meetings, which will be focusing on a particular phrase in the Constitution to help us deal with our environmental plight? Quite simply, we can't be two people, one outside the house and another at home. As a nation, we have but one soul that we have hardened beyond measure by bringing death and imprisonment to so much of the world. At the core of this brutality is the overriding desire of the business elite to expand markets and control resources and labor. The core abroad is also the core at home. Business elite imperatives have become our center, our soul, to the exclusion of deeper core values based upon love and respect for one another. How else can we explain allowing our own children to become so heavily lead exposed and so burdened with excitotoxins and growth hormones in the food supply? "Pressure treated" wood used in our children's playground equipment is allowed to be embedded with arsenic, which results in an exposure with every contact.[21] Where is our decency?

At Article Four meetings where participants use the iron discipline of listening, those insubstantial differences that separate us can be set aside in moments. Racism is unnecessary baggage. Politicians have long encouraged us, for example, to fear one another, especially along racial and class lines, so that they can hide what they've done to the country and still get our votes. They inflame the abortion discussion for the same reason. In fact, men and women who honestly take opposing sides of that issue are simply attempting, in their separate ways, to stake out a position from which to construct, amid the turmoil, a world with true and lasting human values. I believe that all people who attend Article Four meetings, from whatever background, are likely to find that constructive compromise is possible within the framework of the domestic violence clause.

Implementing the domestic violence clause is a life affirming project. If done well, we, as a nation, can literally choose life instead of death–as religious imperatives have long required. Stopping the poisoning of our children and the planet is work that will take the best efforts of us all, striving together. That is the *fundamentalism* we have all been looking for–liberal and conservative alike. It involves changing the core of our national being from the cold killer of a business imperative to a core of love and respect. It is, quite simply, living up to real family values and abiding by the truths of our great spiritual leaders–at long last. The meetings will be places to make prayers long forgotten become joyful realities.

CHAPTER 22

FULFILLING THE PROMISE

In a very real sense, you were present at the time of the signing of the Constitution at the end of the summer of 1787. You were there, as well, when the Constitution was ratified by the states two years later. Being a citizen and taxpayer, a deal was struck in your name that was binding upon you and all who will follow you. You became obligated to support, financially and with your obedience to its laws, a central government that didn't exist before. You gave up a great deal of your personal independence as well as the independence of your State so that you could be guaranteed security against threats to your survival. Now it is time to require the fulfillment of that promise. Your security is threatened from within by a condition of Constitutional domestic violence.

The process of collecting on that debt begins in the state legislatures because Article IV, Section 4 (the road map in a time capsule) says: "On application of the legislature," the United States shall protect us against domestic violence. I find it quaint that the framers of the Constitution could only imagine a condition of domestic violence arising in one state at a time. Ours is occurring simultaneously in every state and in much of the world, as well.

Fulfillment of the promise is a herculean task that is far beyond the meager resources and limited jurisdiction of the states. In this regard, state legislatures do all that they must by holding hearings and passing resolutions that call upon the federal government to protect citizens pursuant to Article IV, Section 4, the domestic violence clause. In this regard, doing less is doing more. States can't possibly do the job of protecting us.

From the very beginning of our country, the most vociferous political argument has been between those who advocated states' rights and those who advocated a strong central government. *The argument is over* without either side prevailing. The intervening emergency of a virulent condition of environmental domestic violence requires the temporary ascendance of the federal government while it undertakes unusual measures. At the conclusion of the emergency, we can safely resume the endless debate as between states' rights and federal prerogatives. For now, let the call for state power not be used as a refuge for those who wish to avoid responsibilities in an emergency.

The most significant task for the states to accomplish is the setting up of fair and impartial legislative hearings on the issue of whether a condition of domestic violence exists. Your Article Four meetings will have to be directed toward gathering the necessary proofs and coordinating efforts with other groups who are delving into the same matter. You will be educating yourselves, each other, and the general public. I believe that the case for the existence of an environmental emergency under the Constitution is overwhelming. I believe that responsible state legislators will readily want to be honest and forthright judges of the question. Where there is intransigence and control of legislators by dominant economic interests, Article Four proponents will want to encourage the election of others for those seats so that a full and complete hearing can be had on the issue.

Just that process and that process alone has the potential of raising American public discourse from the inane to a serious level. At the same time, people, as never before, will begin to appreciate the need to be actively involved with the workings of government. Civics, however, is a long forgotten subject among Americans who are presently taught to believe that good governance is a right that comes automatically without vigilance and without involvement.

Once the states, or a significant number of them, conclude by resolution, that a condition of domestic violence under Article IV, Section 4 exists, then a train of events will be set in motion based upon responsibilities inherent in such a finding. First, the government of the United States becomes obligated to deal with that condition of environmental emergency. Article IV, Section 4 does not say that the United States may or should consider protecting the people.

To the contrary, the framers required the federal government to act in the most uncompromising language possible, saying that on application of the state legislatures, the United States *shall protect* us.

Skeptics will say that simply calling words in the Constitution to the attention of the federal government is a long way from getting that level of government to commit itself, heart and soul, to take the actions necessary. Such criticism overlooks the significance of what will necessarily happen in the various state legislatures. The people who advocate the use of Article IV, Section 4 will be a diverse group, united around a common theme. The case they will argue is personal, compelling, and overwhelming. Reaction by significant corporate interests is likely to be heated and negative. Major resources will probably be devoted by certain industries in an effort to thwart changes to the status quo. Legislators, however, will not be asked to spend state money or commit state resources. Being free to decide the question on its merits alone, they are likely to give the matter the judicial type of attention it deserves. This will be a time when citizens petitioning at the state capitols can mobilize public opinion in a way heretofore impossible. When that happens, the federal government is most likely to change the way it functions to meet the tide of public opinion.

It is obvious to me that when the people are divided and otherwise occupied, the federal government takes on a face in the likeness of dominant economic interests. It has been so for so long, that we, the people, have forgotten that government was supposed to reflect our desires. When Article Four meetings spawn strong legislative initiatives in the various states, a movement will be born that has more than enough potential to turn, at long last, the federal government into the servant that it was designed to be. All of that begins with the first words of greetings and good fellowship at your Article Four meetings.

The second item inherent in a finding that a condition of environmental domestic violence exists is that we, not some foreign power, have brought about the harm. It wasn't the much touted Russians or the once feared Chinese. The heedless horsemen who have taken us to the brink of disaster turn out to be our own kind, fully invested with property rights of some sort or another and holding an iron grip on the dual reins of political power and media attention. That simple truth, once internalized by those who constitute the federal government, has the power to bring about changes necessary to make the government and our society "human centered," to borrow the phrase of René Dubos. There has never been and there will never be an enemy of the American people who will come anywhere near matching ourselves for producing such an array of vectors of destruction. From that must all public policy flow.

The third item inherent in a finding of the existence of a condition of environmental domestic violence has to do with the use of government power. If the causes of our despair are internal, then the federal government must, under emergency circumstances and for a limited period of time, take unto itself unusual and special powers with which to deal with the internal affairs that are bringing about that crisis. The situation is no different in concept from the way the federal government has acted during periods of war. Threats to survival, whether from a foreign power by "invasion" or from ourselves by "domestic violence," are both threats to survival. Under normal circumstances, the federal government is one of enumerated and limited powers. It generally does only what it is specifically allowed to do by the Constitution. According to the tenth Amendment to the Constitution, the residue of power rests in the states and with the people. During emergencies, however, the imperatives of survival require that *all* power reside with that level of government that carries the burden of responsibility. Without that gathering in of power, the mandate "shall protect," under Article IV, Section 4 would be a mockery.

Isn't the gathering in of all power into the federal government, albeit with great involvement of the American people, the very antithesis of a human centered government? Don't we normally equate large with impersonal and small with human scale? Of course. Many environmentalists as well as the majority of business leaders urge a less intrusive and a smaller federal government. Conservatives and liberals alike have come to distrust a big central government. Small *is* beautiful. Human centered is the goal. How then can concentrating all power, even for a brief time, be a correct strategy for America? My answer is that it is the *only* strategy by which we can get to a society of human scale and a country that is, at last, human centered. It will take both power and resources to have us change the direction in which our country is headed.

Picture the United States as a one track railroad headed for destruction. To get passengers moving toward safety, new track will have to be laid and the trains will have to be moved onto that new track. At some later time, schedules can be regular, timely, and routine–human centered. For now, the work of changing direction is anything but easily doable by the ordinary passengers. It is costly beyond the normal fare. It is dangerous beyond the mere stepping off the platform and onto the train. It requires the taking of property for roadbeds, an act of audacity that not even the most ardent railroad user could possibly muster. In short, a major shift in the direction of society is little likely to occur without extensive use of the organizing power of a central government.

The best way to fully understand how the creation of a large and powerful federal government can lead to survival and a society based on the needs of humans as a central focus is through a few examples. I have a friend who recalls what it used to be like to peel a carrot when he was a child before the advent of chemically based agriculture. The kitchen would fill with the sweet scent of that carrot. My friend was recalling the fruits of an American agriculture before the soil was destroyed by chemical fertilizers, pesticides, and fungicides. My friend was recalling the taste and smell of a carrot that was produced on a family farm where the soil still had a full complement of minerals, earthworms, and a host of other living creatures that worked in concert to produce a health enhancing carrot.

Agriculture is now big business, turning out foods of inadequate nutrient density on huge farms that depend less on people than on massive and expensive machines and continuous applications of chemicals. As with any successful business, it is fully entrenched against change. Agribusiness, as it has been called, is a combination of some of the largest chemical companies in the world, together with vast land holding corporations, machinery makers, food distribution companies, and financial institutions. Thus constituted, agribusiness controls politics and politicians. Its component parts are major advertisers in the media. As a result, it tells the story of its own greatness in a hundred ways every day to a public that has been brainwashed to feel blessed because of its very existence.

It is true that consumer demand for organic carrots and other foods without pesticides will have some limited effect on the combined business interests known as agribusiness. The basic structure of large, machinery and chemically driven farming, however, is as a result, little likely to change. Chemical companies, beholden to their stockholders, will want to continue distributing their wares to the venture. In like manner, machinery producers will extol the virtues of what they sell to the venture as labor saving devices without which agriculture would be impossible. Food distribution companies will justify adulteration and further processing in order to extend shelf life after extensive handling and cross country shipping. Banks will defend to the last their right to require clauses in lending agreements that demand that farmers use all the pesticides and fungicides necessary to protect against a crop failure that might diminish lender security.

Only the federal government is large enough and potentially strong enough to break the stranglehold of such an enterprise with such massive power and influence. The situation is not unlike the need for trustbusting that existed at the beginning of the 20th century. Only the intelligent use of emergency federal power for a limited amount of time under the domestic violence clause can match the accumulated strength and awesome concentration of property rights of agribusiness as it presently exists. And the federal power can take us to smaller and more local agriculture that produces foods without the poisons and which contains a high enough nutrient density to assure optimal health in the population.

The federal government can do that because it can target resources to match real human needs. Unlike businesses, government does the hard and necessary things that do not entail the simple sale of products at a profit. So, government can mandate an end to chemical farming and require organic methods. It can outlaw bank requirements for the use of chemicals and, itself, guarantee loans during the transition period from chemical to safe farming. Government can even order that the leaves that fall every autumn in and near our cities be collected and used for enrichment of farming soil throughout the United States. Government can break up the large animal feed lots and require that farming include animal husbandry so that its by-products may be used, as well, to enrich the soil. If not saddled by the costs of maintaining a standing army, government can pay us to do that work which no private industry presently wants to accomplish.

The requirement that we only produce healthful foods will, of necessity, benefit and favor smaller farms over larger ones. A return to family farming can be ensured by giving corporate-like status to the organic farm. As long as it is used for that beneficial purpose, it can be exempted, under the domestic violence clause, from all taxes upon transfer to another organic farmer. Foods that can only be moved over long distances and stored for inordinate lengths of time through the use of genetic engineering and damaging chemical processing will simply be outlawed.

In this manner, small farming becomes favored over large farming for purposes of the public health. Without the temporary investing of emergency power in the federal government to accomplish the purpose, it will not happen on the scale necessary. Use of the federal government in that manner can make it occur in a matter of a few short years. My old friend, with our help, can again buy a carrot from his local market that, when peeled, will fill his kitchen with a sweet aroma and deliver on the promise of contributing to vibrant health. The many vectors of ill health that reach us as a result of our present chemicalized agribusiness need not continue; they simply must not be allowed to continue. As the eminent farm policy critic, Wendell Berry, has pointed out, only a return to family farming can assure loving use of the land so that it need not wear out, but may remain productive and life-enhancing indefinitely.[1]

Another example of how a large and powerful central government is required to assure survival and get us to a society based on human needs involves the curbing of wasteful consumerism. At bottom, our actual needs are few and easily met. How much more do we need than good food, safe water, adequate shelter, a guiding spiritual center, intellectual stimulation, work that suits our natures, and a community within which to share ourselves with others? The American "economy," on the other hand, would be considered "sluggish" and "failing" if people were allowed to pursue simple lives of inexpensive and easily met needs. As a result, every day and every hour of the day, the most affluent economic interests in the world are allowed and are encouraged to use enormously sophisticated advertising techniques to make us want more and spend more. We are no match for that unrelenting power arrayed against us in our every waking moment. On islands with a trade wind that blows each day in the same direction, the trees bend and grow in that direction. We are like those trees.

Vance Packard, in his 1960 classic book, *The Waste Makers*, warned that the United States would become a "have-not nation." It could not be otherwise, he said. We were six percent of the world's population, using up more than half of the planet's natural resources that were processed each year. According to Packard, this imbalanced condition was sustained by continuously pressuring the American consumer to purchase goods even though there was no pressing need to be satisfied. Advertising had created a "hyperthyroid economy," driven by fear of economic collapse. We were, as he said, like a nation riding the back of a tiger, not knowing how to stop the animal and fearful that falling off meant our demise.[2] We are still riding the back of that tiger.

Just as American farming is firmly in the grip of large economic interests, so is the production of goods and the creation of false demand for those goods firmly in the grip of large economic interests. Consumer preferences for a simple life that includes owning fewer, but higher quality products have been shattered by withering blasts of advertising. My old friend who likes good carrots has been made to feel that his clothes are out of style long before they are worn out. His children have been led to believe that a certain label on one's jeans is a ticket to social acceptance. His old car still runs, but he'll trade it in soon because he has been made to fear what business associates and neighbors will think about his being seen continuing to drive the old one. He shaves with a plastic razor that he throws out at the end of the week. He has given up his search for a watch that is wound by hand. Those are not made any longer. Instead, he dutifully buys batteries for his watches and throws the used ones out in the garbage, the first step to their polluting his environment.

This home market is dominated by a combine of industrial, financial, and advertising interests that are both national and international in scope. They created the tiger. They feed the tiger. They live off the tiger.

Only the government of the United States, using the domestic violence clause of Article IV, Section 4 of the Constitution, can effectively challenge and temporarily modify those wasteful economic practices. Only big government can stand up to the array of legal rights and economic advantages possessed by the companies that must be made to stand down for the sake of public health and survival. Big government alone can bring us back to a more manageable economy of human scale that is designed to fulfill human and planetary needs. And it can be done so easily, once the political will to accomplish the job is made manifest through expressions that can come from Article Four meetings.

Our present economic practices, based upon waste and no longer affordable on this endangered Earth, are entirely dependent for their very existence upon a constant and undisturbed stream of product advertising. Product advertising on radio, television, newspapers, and magazines pays for and brings us the great bulk of our news, public discussions, and our entertainment. In short, the marketplace has become the purveyor of our culture. To make matters worse, owners of the various media are now also the owners of businesses whose goal it is to maintain the hyperthyroid economy.

The extent to which advertising must be controlled, using the enormous emergency power of the domestic violence clause, is a large discussion to be taken up at length at Article Four meetings. Some will say that allowing the targeting of children was a gross error to begin with. Television advertising aimed at children, for example, may be considered no different from inviting adult salesmen into our living rooms to pitch wares to them in the absence of parents or any supervision. Others might talk about the need for a total separation between our economic and our cultural lives. During this emergency period of time, can we afford the luxury of media that will be bent exclusively on the continuous selling of products instead of directing themselves to educate and mobilize the country to meet our environmental crisis? Should there not be just a large number, for example, of television channels exclusively devoted to commercial messages for all who want to hear them–people who happen to be considering the purchase of a product? Other channels would carry everything else–all that is our culture–undebased by commercial timidity and a narrow business bias. However the debate ends up, the only reason it will not be idle talk is because of the potential power of the domestic violence clause. It alone allows for the possibility of an effective federal government to create an economy of human scale geared for survival instead of destruction.

An unrestricted consumer-based economy can not possibly deal effectively with an emergency that challenges survival. When the bombing of Pearl Harbor by the Japanese on December 7, 1941 signaled a challenge to our security, the consumer economy was forced to give way to federal control. Steel was needed for tanks and could not be used for automobiles. Gasoline and thousands of items formerly in general use were rationed and kept in reserve for the military–for the common defense. The bombing was an easily understood symbol to all Americans that the time for privations and acceptance of federal control had come. In light of the obvious challenge to survival, an unrestricted consumer society was readily relegated to some time in the future, after we could attain victory.

In our own time, the harm that we have done to ourselves has been accomplished in a quieter fashion than the bombing of December 7, 1941. It has, by no means, however, been less damaging. For well over fifty years, we have insidiously violated ourselves with a bombardment of toxins from our conception clear through to our last breath. The results of these insidious violations are all around us all the time. Children with cancer and asthma are victims. Americans who lack the capacity for critical thinking have been thusly violated. The thin veneer that is civilization itself has begun to peel away. A brute society where human life is considered valueless, where killing now regularly takes place for the thrill of it or for a quarter in the cash register is already upon us. And all of this is a consequence of the violence we have so quietly and heedlessly visited upon ourselves.

The most troubling part of this tragedy is that underneath our denial we all know what is happening. When I speak about this subject, it comes as no surprise to audiences that we have so harmed ourselves. Opposition comes from those who either can not or do not want to conceive of the possibility of interference in peace time with the consumer economy. I have come to think of that as a chamber of commerce mentality. It requires that we say nothing and do nothing that might interfere with the public's confidence in the economy and in the desire to freely purchase goods and services. One particular chamber of commerce member cornered me after a public discussion of the domestic violence clause. I had referred to the futility of keeping secret the harm we have done to ourselves through multiple chemical exposures, saying "it is like trying to hold back the wind." His response was typical of those people who fear getting off the tiger of a manipulated hyperthyroid economy. He said: "Sometimes you *can* hold back the wind."

I carry a sadness around with me. I believe it is shared by many people. The signs of an environmental holocaust are clear. Each year that we allow to go by without aggressively dealing with the crisis is a lost opportunity. Even with our heightened Earth consciousness, we may not prevail. Climate changes, increasing population density pressures, and diminishing human intelligence puts us up to bat in the late innings, behind in the score with two strikes against us. My sadness and my fear is that we will succumb to the apocalypse of a brute society on a planet that we shall make uninhabitable without even putting up a fight.

At present, our political system, driven by the dominant economic interests, seems bent on destroying the federal government and reducing it to the status of a powerless debating society, as it was under the Articles of Confederation before the birth of our Constitution. That federal government, now in full retreat, is our only hope of survival. To put it another way, would the federal government be so vilified by the dominant economic interests if it did not have both the responsibility and the capacity to bring about structural changes that are now so necessary? The essential problem for those dominant forces is that they do not readily give up power in the public interest. Civics has little meaning in "bottom line" thinking. Stockholders demand profits. Managers of corporations have job descriptions that never really include factoring in the public good and long term analyses of public health considerations.

The federal government (using emergency powers of the domestic violence clause) is the only player now capable of the heroic activities needed for survival. It can quiet the tiger and gently remove us all safely from its back. It can shelve waste and war. From a civilian dominated Pentagon building can come a plethora of jobs and new industries geared for helping us attain our dignity on this planet and assure our survival. Total concentration on survival will allow us to do many important things at once. When preparing for war, a nation does not make helmets one year and guns the next. The same is true for a nation fighting a battle against domestic violence. All necessary actions, as far as human intelligence and will can allow, are done at once.

It's not the purpose of this book to lay out a step by step plan of action, but I would be remiss in not going through a few ideas for action, in addition to those already discussed in previous chapters. Fulfillment of the promise contained in the domestic violence clause will require a transformation of the federal government from a fiefdom largely controlled by the dominant economic interests to being a true public servant. Much of that changeover can be started simply by executive order of the President of the United States, without the need for the passage of laws. Indeed, such a metamorphosis will *require* a jump-start by a strong president, emboldened by a public outcry for use of emergency provisions pursuant to the domestic violence clause. The boldness and strength of President Lincoln comes to mind, when in 1861 at the outbreak of the Civil War, he took it upon himself to suspend the writ of habeas corpus throughout the land. "We have a case of rebellion," Lincoln wrote to the protesting Chief Justice Taney, and survival requires suspension of the normal rules of due process.[3]

I do not suggest that anything near as drastic as Lincoln's doing away with an accused's right to a trial by jury be accomplished by executive order. There are, however, simple and decent things that can be ordered in a moment—changes which can transform government itself and make it once again an institution worthy of the respect of all. Without that respect, government is incapable of leadership.

President Smith—let's give him or her a name—can, for example, order that no one in the entire executive branch have contact with lobbyists without immediately making public exactly what was discussed. We live in an age where instant communication is possible. I can think of no better use for that technology.

President Smith can dismantle, by executive order, the secret government that includes the CIA, the various military intelligence services, and that portion of the FBI that insists on punishing free speech and imaginative thought. In doing so, the president would speak for me by apologizing as well for all the foolishness and the suffering caused at home and around the world by our using those covert and illegal forces for the benefit of business interests. Time and again, those covert and illegal forces have protected businesses that cause environmental destruction and bring about the importation of toxic-laden products for consumption in the home market. The world is too small to consider degradation elsewhere to be an isolated event.

We no longer elect a president of just our country. Owing to the fact that the United States is militarily unrivaled in the world, we elect what should be considered the first citizen of the world. Recognizing the existence of an emergency condition of domestic violence in the United States, our President Smith can order a halt to the production, sale, and export of all military goods. I believe by being shown that example other nations will follow suit. Put another way, disarmament and the transition of resources for the purposes of environmental and health protection on a global scale can not take place unless and until our President exerts that leadership. The process can so easily start with our Mr. or Ms. Smith. Abraham Lincoln did not become a respected leader by following a well worn path pointed out to him by his predecessors. He had the courage to publicly recognize and oppose the moral wrong of his day—slavery.[4] Is not the moral wrong of our day—destruction of the Earth—as easy to recognize and to oppose? If slavery, as Lincoln said, would result in the evil of a "house divided,"[5] is not the evil we face all the greater—a

183

house made unlivable, a planet in ruin, and its people forced into inhuman and brute societies?

Without the burden of carrying a standing army and without the waste of an unrestricted consumer-based economy, the federal government can truly embark on the task of tending to the public health pursuant to Article IV, Section 4. Manufacturing companies, instead of just being bullied into compliance with various air and water pollution standards, will be helped to reach zero discharge. Money grants and technical assistance for that purpose can be made available to all companies, large and small. The cleanup of the country, hardly even begun under the so-called "Superfund," can begin in earnest under the domestic violence clause. We have so thoroughly degraded our environment that there is work enough for two generations–work of the most fulfilling kind, the doing of which we were put on this Earth to accomplish.

Fifty years from now, when we will have transformed so many of our institutions, from the way health care occurs to the way the market place operates, we will look back on all the work done to assure survival. My children and yours will, no doubt, express gratitude for the wisdom of the framers of the Constitution. They knew we would be our own worst enemy and had the foresight to give us a roadmap in a time capsule to find our way back to a safe haven. Having used that roadmap, we will be able to respond to Benjamin Franklin's caution: Yes, the Earth is yet inhabitable, and there is health and vitality in all who now walk lightly upon it, respecting its fragility and understanding our vital connection to it. Yes, we have been able to keep it.

REFERENCES

CHAPTER 1: INTRODUCTIONS

1. James Gleick, "Part Showman, All Genius," *New York Times Magazine*, Sept. 20, 1992, page 39, at page 44.

2. René Dubos, *Mirage of Health: Utopias, Progress, and Biological Change* (New Brunswick, N. J.: Rutgers University Press, 1987), pages 53-55.

3. James Madison, *Notes of Debates in the Federal Convention Of 1787 Reported by James Madison* (Athens, Ohio: Ohio University Press, 1984), pages 214-215.

CHAPTER 2: CORNERSTONE OF THE CONSTITUTION

1. Marion Starkey, *A Little Rebellion* (New York: Alfred A. Knopf, 1955), page 130.

2. Carl Van Doren, *The Great Rehearsal: The Story of the Making and Ratifying of the Constitution of the United States* (New York: Viking Press, 1948), pages 9-23.

3. James Madison, *Notes of Debates*, pages 28-30.

4. James Madison, *Notes of Debates*, page 28.

CHAPTER 3: WHAT THEY MEANT BY DOMESTIC VIOLENCE

1. Catherine Drinker Bowen, *Miracle at Philadelphia: The Story of the Constitutional Convention May to September 1787* (Boston: Little, Brown and Company, 1966), page 197.

2. *Proceedings of the Massachusetts Historical Society of 1884 and 1885* (Boston, 1885), 2nd. ser., vol. 1, pages 298-303.

3. Marion Starkey, *A Little Rebellion*, pages 132 and 172.

4. *Oxford English Dictionary*, 1933, s.v. "violence, violency, violent, violently, and violentness."

5. *Federalist*, No. 6.

6. James Madison, *Notes of Debates*, page 560.

7. William Shakespeare, *King Richard II*, Act 3, Scene 2, line 147.

CHAPTER 4: IF YOU CAN KEEP IT

1. *Bartlett's Familiar Quotations*, 16th ed. (Boston: Little, Brown and Company, 1992), page 310.

2. Merrill Jensen, *The New Nation: A History of the United States During the Confederation, 1781-1789* (New York: Alfred A. Knopf, 1967), page 233.

3. Merrill Jensen, *The New Nation*, page 289.

4. Merrill Jensen, *The New Nation*, pages 152-153.

5. Daniel Yergin, *The Prize: The Epic Quest for Oil, Money, and Power* (New York: Simon and Schuster, 1991), page 27.

6. Graham D. Taylor and Patricia E. Sudnik, *DuPont and the International Chemical Industry* (Boston: Twayne Publishers, 1984), pages 43-58.

7. John B. Rae, *Henry Ford* (Englewood Cliffs, N. J.: Prentice-Hall, 1969), page 67.

8. James M. Fallows, *The Water Lords*, Foreword by Ralph Nader (New York: Grossman Publishers, 1971), page xi.

9. Lester R. Brown and Edward C. Wolf, "Charting a Sustainable Course," *State of the World 1987: A Worldwatch Institute Report on Progress Toward a Sustainable Society*, ed. Linda Starke (New York: W. W. Norton and Co., 1987), page 213.

CHAPTER 5: A CLAUSE FOR THE PEOPLE

1. *Texas v. White*, 74 U. S. (7 Wall.) 700 (1868).

2. *Colegrove v. Green*, 328 U. S. 549 (1946), at page 556.

3. Clarence C. Ferguson, "The Inherent Justiciability of the Constitutional Guaranty Against Domestic Violence," 13 *Rutgers Law Review* 407 (1959). William L. Wiecek, *The Guarantee Clause of the U. S. Constitution* (Ithaca: Cornell University Press, 1972), pages 264-289.

CHAPTER 6: A CONDITION OF DOMESTIC VIOLENCE

1. René Dubos, "The Limits of Adaptability," *The Environmental Handbook*, ed. Garrett DeBell (New York: Ballantine Books, 1970), pages 28-29.

REFERENCES

2. Phillip M. Boffey, "Breast Cancer Continues Gradual Rise," *New York Times,* Feb. 2, 1988, page C1.

3. "Action Urged on Ozone-Destroying Chemicals," *Star-Ledger* (Newark, N. J.), March 10, 1988, page 11 and telephone interview of Dr. Darrel Rigel on July 5, 1988.

4. Dr. Walter Burnstein, from a speech given in Linden, N. J., November, 1985.

5. *Rachel's Hazardous Waste News,* Jan. 30, 1991.

6. James Barron, "Suicide Rates of Teen-Agers: Are Their Lives Harder to Live?" *New York Times,* April 15, 1987, page C1.

7. Charles Patrick Ewing, *Kids Who Kill* (Lexington, Mass.: Lexington Books, 1990), page 157. Daniel Goleman, "Brain Defect Tied to Utter Amorality of the Psychopath," *New York Times,* July 7, 1987, page C1.

8. Harold M. Schmeck, Jr., "Brain Defects Seen in Those Who Repeat Violent Acts," *New York Times,* Sept. 17, 1985, page C1.

9. Sam Howe Verhovek, "In Wake of Drive-By Shootings, Texas Contractor Sells Bullet Shields for Homes," *New York Times,* July 11, 1994, page 13.

10. "Students Termed Weak on Writing. Report Says the Young Lack Thinking Skills Needed in an Advanced Society," *New York Times,* Dec. 4, 1986, page 26. Edward B. Fiske, "Literacy in America: Beyond the Basics," *New York Times,* Sept. 26, 1986, page 15.

11. René Dubos, "The Limits of Adaptability," pages 28-29.

12. Barbara Tuchman, "A Nation in Decline," *New York Times Magazine,* Aug. 20, 1987, page 52.

13. Louis V. Gerstner, Jr., "Our Schools Are Failing: Do We Care?" *New York Times,* May 27, 1994, page 27, op-ed.

14. Richard B. Morris, *Seven Who Shaped Our Destiny* (New York: Harper and Row, 1973), page 1.

15. Barbara Tuchman, *The March of Folly: From Troy to Vietnam* (New York: Alfred A. Knopf, 1984).

16. Jack London, *The People of the Abyss,* in *Jack London* (New York: Exeter Books, 1986), pages 664-665.

17. Joyce Carol Oates, "Family," *Omni,* Dec. 1989, page 74.

18. William Broad and Nicholas Wade, *Betrayers of the Truth: Fraud and Deceit in the Halls of Science* (New York: Simon and Schuster, 1982), page 219.

19. Spencer Klaw, *The New Brahmins: Scientific Life in America* (New York: William Morrow and Co., 1968), pages 106-107.

20. Robert Bell, *Impure Science: Fraud, Compromise, and Political Influence in Scientific Research* (New York: John Wiley and Sons, 1992), page 248.

21. Albert Einstein, *Ideas and Opinions* (New York: Dell Publishing Co., 1973), pages 219-222.

22. William Broad and Nicholas Wade, *Betrayers of the Truth*, page 223.

CHAPTER 7: THE GOOD NEWS

1. Donald E. Carr, *The Sky Is Still Falling* (New York: W. W. Norton and Co., 1982), pages 37-38 and 40-41.

2. Jane E. Brody, "Aggressiveness and Delinquency In Boys Is Linked to Lead in Bones," *New York Times*, Feb. 7, 1996, page C9.

3. Herbert L. Needleman and Sergio Piomelli, *The Effects of Low Level Lead Exposure* (New York: Natural Resources Defense Council, 1978), page 4.

4. "Researchers Report Lead in Modern Man is High," *New York Times*, April 27, 1979, page 14.

5. Matt Clark, "Here's Lead in Your Wine," *Newsweek*, March 28, 1983, page 53.

6. Lewis Regenstein, *America the Poisoned* (Washington, D. C.: Acropolis Books, 1982), page 258.

7. Genesis 41: 1-50.

8. *The Torah, A Modern Commentary* (New York: The Union of American Hebrew Congregations, 1981), page 272.

CHAPTER 8: PUTTING RESOURCES INTO EDUCATION

1. R. W. Thatcher et al., "Effects of Low Levels of Cadmium and Lead on Cognitive Functioning in Children," *Archives of Environmental Health*, vol. 37, pages 159-166, May/June 1982.

2. *Federalist*, No. 6.

3. *Federalist*, No. 31.

4. Brenda Eskenazi, "Behavioral Teratology," in *Perinatal Epidemiology*, ed. Michael B. Bracken (New York: Oxford Press, 1984), page 217.

5. René Dubos, "Is This Progress...Or Self Destruction?" *New York Times*, Jan. 6, 1969, page 142.

6. Richard D. Lyons, "Physical and Mental Disabilities In Newborns Doubled in 25 Years," *New York Times*, July 18, 1983, page 1. Newacheck, Budetti, and

REFERENCES

McManus, "Trends in Childhood Disability," *American Journal of Public Health*, vol. 74, pages 232-236, 1984.

7. New Jersey Department of Education, *Special Education: A Statistical Report for the 1983-1984 School Year*, Trenton, October 1984, Introduction.

8. "Study Casts Doubt on Reforms as Key to Improved Student Performance," *Star-Ledger* (Newark, N. J.), Aug. 24, 1987, page 9.

9. Jane M. Healy, *Endangered Minds: Why Our Children Don't Think* (New York: Simon and Schuster, 1990), pages 27-29.

CHAPTER 9: IMPROVING IN THE WORKPLACE

1. Herbert L. Needleman and Sergio Piomelli, *The Effects of Low Level Lead Exposure* (New York: Natural Resources Defense Council, 1978), page 20.

2. Daniel Goleman, "Peril Is Seen for Babies Whose Mothers Ate Fish With PCBs," *New York Times*, July 22, 1984, page 16.

3. Richard J. Wurtman, "Why No Testing of Additives?" *New York Times*, Dec. 23, 1987, page 23.

4. Marian Burros, "Residue of Chemicals in Meat Leads to Debate on Hazards," *New York Times*, March 15, 1983, page 1.

5. Joseph Chilton Pearce, *Evolution's End: Claiming the Potential of Our Intelligence* (San Francisco: Harper, 1992), pages 198-201.

6. "Science Watch: Cadmium and Alcoholism," *New York Times*, Aug. 4, 1987, page C6 and telephone conversation with Dr. Nation in Sept., 1988.

7. Janice Simpson, "A Shallow Labor Pool Spurs Business to Act to Bolster Education," *Wall Street Journal*, Sept. 28, 1987, page 1.

8. "The Pollution of the Great Lakes," Part III, broadcast by National Public Radio on *All Things Considered* and *Morning Edition* in March, 1984, transcript page 4.

9. Michael Keating, "Thin Blanket of Pesticides Called Threat," *Globe and Mail* (Toronto, Canada), Oct. 31, 1987, page 13.

10. Peter Calamai, *Broken Words: Why Five Million Canadians Are Illiterate*, ed. Norm Ovenden (Toronto: Southam Newspaper Group, 1987), pages 7 and 13.

11. Peter Calamai, *Broken Words*, page 58.

12. "Great Lakes Ranked As Most Toxic Area," *Star-Ledger* (Newark, N. J.), Dec. 12, 1985, page 84.

13. Wayne Schmidt, "Great Lakes Cleanup 'Miracle' Appears Stalled," *Star-Ledger* (Newark, N. J.), Nov. 17, 1986, page 13.

14. Wayne Hearn, "The Ailing Great Lakes," *Star-Ledger* (Newark, N. J.), Aug. 31, 1987, page 13.

15. Louis V. Gerstner, Jr., "Our Schools Are Failing: Do We Care?" *New York Times*, May 27, 1994, page 27, op-ed.

CHAPTER 10: GETTING TO BE SAFE AT HOME

1. Lisa Belkin, "Experts Find Air Pollution In the Home a Growing Risk," *New York Times*, March 7, 1985, page C1.

2. Arthur M. Schlessinger, Jr., *The Cycles of American History* (Boston: Houghton Miflin Co., 1986), pages 132-136.

3. A. Cressy Morrison, *Man in a Chemical World: The Service of Chemical Industry* (New York: Charles Scribner's Sons, 1937), pages 250 and 283.

4. Daniel Ford, *The Cult of the Atom* (New York: Simon and Schuster, Touchstone Ed., 1982), page 14.

5. William Greider, *Who Will Tell the People* (New York: Simon and Schuster, Touchstone Ed., 1993), page 39.

6. Joseph Chilton Pearce, *Evolution's End: Claiming the Potential of Our Intelligence* (San Francisco: Harper, 1992), pages 198 and 241, note 2.

7. Isabel Wilkerson, "2 Boys, a Debt, a Gun, a Victim: The Face of Violence," *New York Times*, May 16, 1994, page 1 and page 14, paragraph 5.

8. Keith Schneider, "F. D. A. Warns the Dairy Industry Not to Label Milk Hormone-Free," *New York Times*, Feb. 8, 1994, page 1.

9. Isabel Wilkerson, "2 Boys, a Debt, a Gun, a Victim: The Face of Violence," *New York Times*, May 16, 1994, page 1.

10. "Common Bacteria Said to Be Turning Untreatable," *New York Times*, Feb. 20, 1994, page 24.

11. James Barron, "E. Coli Bacteria Sicken Five More in New Jersey," *New York Times*, July 23, 1994, page 25.

12. Spencer Reiss and Nina Archer Biddle, "The Strep-A Scare," *Newsweek*, June 20, 1994, page 32. Sheryl Stolberg, "Killer Bug Perfect for Prime Time," *Los Angeles Times*, June 15, 1994, page 1.

13. John T. McQuiston, "Two Hospitalized With Life-Threatening Form of Strep Throat," *New York Times*, June 6, 1994, page B5.

14. Andrew Nikiforuk, *The Fourth Horseman* (New York: M. Evans and Co., 1991), pages 180-181.

15. Keith Schneider, "Fetal Harm, Not Cancer, Is Called The Primary Threat From Dioxin," *New York Times*, May 11, 1994, page 1.

16. Rachel Carson, *Silent Spring* (New York: Houghton Mifflin, 1962), pages 85-100 and 258-261.

17. Timothy Aeppel, "'Safe' Pesticides Polluting Environment-Echoes From the 'Silent Spring'," *Christian Science Monitor*, July 20, 1987, page 1.

18. Philip Shabecoff, "'Silent Spring' Led to Safer Pesticides, But Use Is Up," *New York Times*, April 21, 1986, page 14.

19. Lawrie Mott and Karen Snyder, *Pesticide Alert: A Guide to Pesticides in Fruits and Vegetables* (San Francisco: Sierra Club Books, 1987), page 30.

20. "Chemicals in the News: Insecticides," *New Jersey Hazardous Waste News*, June/Aug. 1985, page 2.

21. Timothy Aeppel, "'Safe' Pesticides Polluting Environment."

22. *Federalist*, No. 10.

23. *Federalist*, No. 51.

24. *Federalist*, No. 10.

25. William Greider, *Who Will Tell the People* (New York: Simon and Schuster, 1993), page 66.

26. William Wiecek, *The Guarantee Clause of the U. S. Constitution* (Ithaca: Cornell University Press, 1972), pages 168, 214, and 290.

CHAPTER 11: A SELF EXAMINATION

1. William Greider, *Who Will Tell the People*, pages 66 and 87-88.

2. Michael Kamen, *A Machine That Would Go of Itself* (New York: Alfred A. Knopf, 1987), pages 3-4.

3. *Federalist*, No. 10.

4. *The Quotation Dictionary*, ed. Robin Hyman (New York: The Macmillan Company, 1962), page 144.

CHAPTER 12: OPTIMAL HEALTH

1. Sandra Blakeslee, "Gene Transplant Speeds Salmon Growth Rate," *New York Times*, Sept. 20, 1994, page C6.

2. Michael Diamond, "Battling the Unrecognized Toxic Enemy," a letter to the editor, *Star-Ledger* (Newark, N. J.), July 25, 1983, page 15.

3. Dr. Bernard Goldstein, "Forum on the Environment," Westfield, N. J., Dec. 13, 1984.

4. Associated Press, "New Fears on Chemicals and Nervous System," *New York Times*, May 17, 1990, page 17.

5. "E. P. A. Urged to Broaden Air Pollution Studies," *New York Times*, May 28, 1991, page C4.

6. Judges 13: 4 and 14.

7. *Encyclopaedia Judaica*, corrected ed., s.v. "Dietary Laws." *The New Schaff-Herzog Encyclopedia of Religious Knowledge*, fifth printing, s.v. "Dietary Laws of the Hebrews."

8. Judges 13: 5.

CHAPTER 13: THE ROAD TO OPTIMAL HEALTH

1. Bernie Siegel, *Love, Medicine and Miracles* (New York: Harper and Row, 1986), pages 148-150.

2. Lee Botts, Professor at Northwestern University, interviewed on "The Pollution of the Great Lakes," Part III, broadcast by National Public Radio on *All Things Considered* and *Morning Edition* in March, 1984, transcript page 4.

3. Debra Lynn Dadd, *The Nontoxic Home and Office* (Los Angeles: Jeremy P. Tarcher, Inc., 1992), pages 13-14 and 36.

4. Harris L. Coulter, *Divided Legacy: The Conflict Between Homeopathy and the American Medical Association* (Berkeley: North Atlantic Books, 1982), pages 87-101 and 506-509.

5. Philip Shabecoff, "New Safeguards for Home Pesticides Debated," *New York Times*, May 11, 1986, page 26.

6. Warren Schultz, *The Chemical Free Lawn* (Emmaus, Penn.: Rodale Press, 1989). *Lawn Beauty the Organic Way*, ed. J. I. Rodale (Emmaus: Rodale Books, 1970). Franklin Stuart, *Building a Healthy Lawn* (Pownel, Vermont: Storey Communications, 1988).

7. Sara Stein, *Noah's Garden: Restoring the Ecology of Our Own Back Yards* (Boston: Houghton Mifflin, 1993).

8. Sara Stein, *Noah's Garden,* page 18.

9. Sara Stein, *Noah's Garden,* page 136.

10. Sara Stein, *Noah's Garden,* page 26.

REFERENCES

CHAPTER 14: COMMUNITY

1. Peter McDonough, *Men Astutely Trained* (New York: The Free Press, 1992), page xiv.

2. *Federalist*, No. 10.

CHAPTER 15: SWORDS INTO PLOWSHARES

1. "...and they shall beat their swords into plowshares, and their spears into pruninghooks: nation shall not lift up sword against nation, neither shall they learn war any more." Isaiah 2: 4 and Micah 4: 3.

2. Kenneth M. Jensen, ed., *Origins of the Cold War: The Novikov, Kennan, and Roberts "Long Telegrams" of 1946*, rev. ed. (Washington, D. C.: United States Institute of Peace Press, 1993), page 29. All references are to the revised edition, except note 14.

3. Kenneth M. Jensen, ed., *Origins of the Cold War*, pages 24-25.

4. Kenneth M. Jensen, ed., *Origins of the Cold War*, preface to the 1st ed. by Samuel W. Lewis, pages xi-xii.

5. Kenneth M. Jensen, ed., *Origins of the Cold War*, page 17.

6. Kenneth M. Jensen, ed., *Origins of the Cold War*, page 29.

7. Kenneth M. Jensen, ed., *Origins of the Cold War*, pages 17-18.

8. Kenneth M. Jensen, ed., *Origins of the Cold War*, page 18.

9. John Lukacs, *A History of the Cold War* (Garden City, New York: Anchor Books, 1962), page 19, as an example of dismissive treatment of U. S. involvement in the Russian Civil War.

10. Robert K. Massie, *Nicholas and Alexandra: An Intimate Account of the Last of the Romanovs and the Fall of Imperial Russia* (New York: Atheneum, 1967), pages 306-307.

11. W. Bruce Lincoln, *Red Victory: A History of the Russian Civil War* (New York: Simon and Schuster, 1989) and telephone interview of the author on Dec. 13, 1994.

12. Kenneth M. Jensen, ed., *Origins of the Cold War*, page 64.

13. Bill Moyers, *The Secret Government* (Cabin John, Maryland: Seven Locks Press, 1988), foreword by Henry Steele Commager, page xv.

14. Kenneth M. Jensen, ed., *Origins of the Cold War*, preface to the 1st ed. by Samuel W. Lewis, page xiii.

15. Kenneth M. Jensen, ed., *Origins of the Cold War*, 1st ed., facing copyright page.

16. Kenneth M. Jensen, ed., *Origins of the Cold War*, page xix.

17. Kenneth M. Jensen, ed., *Origins of the Cold War*, pages 5-6.

18. Kenneth M. Jensen, ed., *Origins of the Cold War*, pages 6-7.

19. Kenneth M. Jensen, ed., *Origins of the Cold War*, page 7.

20. Kenneth M. Jensen, ed., *Origins of the Cold War*, page 8.

21. Kenneth M. Jensen, ed., *Origins of the Cold War*, page 8 and note 5 on page 69.

22. Kenneth M. Jensen, ed., *Origins of the Cold War*, page 3.

23. Kenneth M. Jensen, ed., *Origins of the Cold War*, page 15.

24. Kenneth M. Jensen, ed., *Origins of the Cold War*, page 16.

25. Paul Kennedy, *The Rise and Fall of the Great Powers* (New York: Vintage Books, 1987), page 392.

26. William Appleman Williams, "Conclusion: The Critics of the American Empire Open a Door to Create an American Community," *From Colony to Empire: Essays in the History of American Foreign Relations*, ed. William Appleman Williams (New York: John Wiley and Sons, 1972), page 485.

27. Scott L. Bills, *Empire and Cold War* (New York: St. Martins Press, 1990), page 210.

28. William Appleman Williams, "Conclusion," page 485.

29. Scott L. Bills, *Empire*, pages 204 and 210.

30. Frederick S. Calhoun, *Uses of Force* (Kent, Ohio: Kent State University Press, 1993), pages 136 and 139.

31. Scott L. Bills, *Empire*, page 208.

32. Scott L. Bills, *Empire*, page 205.

33. Scott L. Bills, *Empire*, pages 204-205. John M. Dower, *War Without Mercy* (New York: Pantheon Books, 1986), page 14.

34. Melvin Gurtov and Ray Maghroori, *Roots of Failure* (Westport, Conn.: Greenwood Press, 1984), pages 9 and 15. See also Claude Julien, *America's Empire* (New York: Pantheon Books, 1971), pages 23-24.

35. Howard Zinn, *A People's History of the United States* (New York: Harper Perennial, 1990), page 416.

36. Center for Defense Information, *The Cost of War in the Post-Cold War Age: Facts on Military Spending* (Washington, D. C., 1994), page 5.

CHAPTER 16: EARTHCEDING

1. Reuters, Washington, D. C., "New Evidence Ties Ozone Hole to Human Activity," *New York Times*, Dec. 20, 1994, page C7.

2. Malcolm W. Browne, "Most Precise Gauge Yet Points to Global Warming," *New York Times*, Dec. 20, 1994, page C4.

3. Ralph F. Keeling, "Measuring Correlations Between Atmospheric Oxygen and Carbon Dioxide Mole Fractions: A Preliminary Study in Urban Air," *Journal of Atmospheric Chemistry*, vol. 7 (1988), 153-176, page 153. Jonathan Weiner, "Global Warming is Still Hot. Ask the Keelings, First Family of the Greenhouse Effect," *New York Times Magazine*, Oct. 23, 1994, page 56.

4. Marlise Simons, "Cousteau, at 83, Emphasizes the Most Important Species: Mankind," *New York Times*, Jan. 30, 1994, page 12.

5. Marlise Simons, "Vast Amazon Fires, Man-Made, Linked to Global Warming," *New York Times*, Aug. 12, 1988, page 1.

6. Reuters, Washington, D. C., "Environmental Refugees at 10 Million," *Star-Ledger* (Newark, N. J.), Nov. 20, 1988, page 80.

7. Mark A. Uhlig, "Mexico City's Toxic Residue Worsens Already Filthy Air," *New York Times*, May 12, 1991, page 1.

8. Barbara Crossette, "300 Factories Add Up to India's Very Sick Town," *New York Times*, Feb. 6, 1991, page 4.

9. Albert Gore, *Earth in the Balance* (Boston: Houghton Mifflin, 1992), page 31.

10. Daniel Goleman, "Insights Into Self-Deception," *New York Times Magazine*, May 12, 1985, pages 36 and 38.

11. Abraham Lincoln, "Annual Message to Congress," Dec. 1, 1862, *Abraham Lincoln: His Speeches and Writings*, ed. Roy P. Bassler (New York: Da Capo Press, 1946), page 688.

12. James Brooke, "A Death in the Amazon, From Symbol to Script," *New York Times*, April 12, 1989, page 4.

13. *Current Biography 1971*, ed. Charles Moritz (New York: H. H. Wilson Co., 1971), page 6.

14. Bill Gulley and Mary Ellen Reese, *Breaking Cover* (New York: Simon and Schuster, 1980), pages 239-240.

15. Victor Marchetti and John D. Marks, *The CIA and the Cult of Intelligence* (New York: Dell Publishing Co., 1974), pages 12, 48, and 319. Melvin Gurtov and Ray Maghroori, *Roots of Failure* (Westport, Conn.: Greenwood Press, 1984), page 23.

16. Morton Mintz and Jerry S. Cohen, *Power Inc.* (New York: Viking Press, 1976), pages 31-32 and 369. Victor Marchetti and John D. Marks, *The CIA and the Cult of Intelligence*, page 13.

17. Victor Marchetti and John D. Marks, *The CIA and the Cult of Intelligence*, page 18.

18. Bob Woodward, *Veil: The Secret Wars of the CIA 1981-1987* (New York: Simon and Schuster, 1987), page 56.

19. Victor Marchetti and John D. Marks, *The CIA and the Cult of Intelligence*, page 18.

20. Victor Marchetti and John D. Marks, *The CIA and the Cult of Intelligence*, page 300.

21. Victor Marchetti and John D. Marks, *The CIA and the Cult of Intelligence*, page 17.

22. Victor Marchetti and John D. Marks, *The CIA and the Cult of Intelligence*, page 17.

23. Howard Zinn, *A People's History of the United States* (New York: Harper Perennial, 1990), page 557.

24. Jacobo Timerman, *Chile: Death in the South* (New York: Alfred A. Knopf, 1987), pages 8, 21, and 29.

25. Jacobo Timerman, *Chile*, pages 27-33.

26. Edward S. Herman and Noam Chomsky, *Manufacturing Consent* (New York: Pantheon Books, 1988), page 33.

27. Noam Chomsky, *Towards a New Cold War* (New York: Pantheon Books, 1982), pages 7-8. Jacobo Timerman, *Chile*, pages 132-133.

28. Victor Marchetti and John D. Marks, *The CIA and the Cult of Intelligence*, page 17.

CHAPTER 17: IN THE SPIRIT OF 1787

1. John le Carré, "The Shame of the West," *New York Times*, Dec. 14, 1994, page 23, op-ed.

2. Tom A. Hudgens, *Let's Abolish War* (Denver: BILR Corp., 1986), page 42.

3. Abraham Lincoln, "Annual Message to Congress," Dec. 1, 1862, *Abraham Lincoln: His Speeches and Writings*, ed. Roy P. Bassler (New York: Da Capo Press, 1946), page 688.

4. Carl Van Doren, *The Great Rehearsal: The Story of the Making and Ratifying of the Constitution of the United States* (New York: Viking Press, 1948), pages viii, x, and 31.

CHAPTER 18: RECLAIMING IMAGINATION

1. Claude G. Bowers, *The Tragic Era: The Revolution After Lincoln* (Cambridge: Riverside Press, 1929), page v.

2. Robert Rienow and Leona Train Rienow, *Of Snuff, Sin, and the Senate* (Chicago: Follett Publishing Company, 1965), pages 280-283.

3. Robert Rienow and Leona Train Rienow, *Of Snuff*, pages 240-244.

4. Robert Rienow and Leona Train Rienow, *Of Snuff*, pages 109-124.

5. Robert Rienow and Leona Train Rienow, *Of Snuff*, page 303.

6. Robert Rienow and Leona Train Rienow, *Of Snuff*, page 307.

7. Robert Rienow and Leona Train Rienow, *Of Snuff*, pages 126, 137-143, 290, and 305.

8. Samuel Eliot Morison, *The Oxford History of the American People* (New York: New American Library, 1972), vol. 3, pages 130-132.

9. Robert K. Massie, *Nicholas and Alexandra: An Intimate Account of the Last of the Romanovs and the Fall of Imperial Russia* (New York: Atheneum, 1967), pages 64-65.

10. Samuel Eliot Morison, *The Oxford History*, vol. 3, page 132.

11. Fred J. Cook, *The FBI Nobody Knows* (New York: The Macmillan Company, 1964), pages 78-80.

12. Fred J. Cook, *The FBI Nobody Knows*, page 78.

13. Fred J. Cook, *The FBI Nobody Knows*, pages 78-93.

14. James Munves, *The FBI and the CIA: Secret Agents and American Democracy* (New York: Harcourt Brace Jovanovich, 1975), page 22.

15. Frank J. Donner, *The Age of Surveillance* (New York: Alfred A. Knopf, 1980), page 3.

16. Herbert Mitgang, *Dangerous Dossiers: Exposing the Secret War Against America's Greatest Authors* (New York: Donald I. Fine, Inc., 1988), pages 87-92.

17. Herbert Mitgang, *Dangerous Dossiers*, pages 61-71.

18. Herbert Mitgang, *Dangerous Dossiers*, page 51.

19. Herbert Mitgang, *Dangerous Dossiers*, pages 183-189.

20. Herbert Mitgang, *Dangerous Dossiers*, page 117.

21. Herbert Mitgang, *Dangerous Dossiers*, pages 164-171.

22. Herbert Mitgang, *Dangerous Dossiers*, pages 203-204.

23. David Wise, "Covert Operations Abroad: An Overview," *The CIA File*, ed. Robert L. Borosage and John Marks (New York: Grossman Publishers, 1976), page 21. Howard Zinn, *A People's History of the United States* (New York: Harper Perennial, 1990), pages 430-431. Stephen Goode, *The CIA* (New York: Franklin Watts, 1982), pages 56-60.

24. Tim Weiner, "Guatemalan Agent of C. I. A. Tied to Killing of American," *New York Times*, March 23, 1995, page 1.

25. Allan Nairn, "C. I. A. Death Squad," *The Nation*, April 17, 1995, pages 511-513.

26. Roger Morris and Richard Mauzy, "Following the Scenario: Reflections on Five Case Histories in the Mode and Aftermath of CIA Intervention," *The CIA File*, ed. Robert L. Borosage and John Marks, pages 33-35.

27. Richard Barnett, "The 'Dirty Tricks' Gap," *The CIA File*, ed. Robert L. Borosage and John Marks, pages 221-222.

28. Thomas B. Ross, "Surreptitious Entry: The CIA's Operations in the United States," *The CIA File*, ed. Robert L. Borosage and John Marks, pages 102-106.

29. David Wise, "Covert Operations Abroad," *The CIA File*, ed. Robert L. Borosage and John Marks, pages 21-22.

30. Elaine Sciolino, "C. I. A. Asks Congress for Money to Rein In Iraq and Iran," *New York Times*, April 12, 1995, page 8.

31. Howard Zinn, *A People's History of the United States* (New York: Harper Perennial, 1990), pages 416-417.

32. Richard Hofstadter, *Anti-intellectualism in American Life* (New York: Vintage Books, 1962), pages 38-45.

33. Thomas B. Ross, "Surreptitious Entry," *The CIA File*, ed. Robert L. Borosage and John Marks, pages 94-95 and 99-100.

34. Sigmund Diamond, *Compromised Campus: The Collaboration of Universities With the Intelligence Community, 1945-1955* (New York: Oxford University Press, 1992), pages 3 and 25.

35. Thomas B. Ross, "Surreptitious Entry," page 103.

36. Thomas B. Ross, "Surreptitious Entry," page 97.

37. Thomas B. Ross, "Surreptitious Entry," page 102.

38. Thomas B. Ross, "Surreptitious Entry," page 102.

39. Herbert Mitgang, *Dangerous Dossiers*, pages 298-299.

40. Thomas B. Ross, "Surreptitious Entry," page 100.

41. Sigmund Diamond, *Compromised Campus*, pages 275-276.

42. Howard Zinn, *A People's History of the United States*, pages 420-421.

43. Charles Goodell, *Political Prisoners in America* (New York: Random House, 1973), pages 90-97.

44. Charles Goodell, *Political Prisoners*, pages 129-130.

45. R. W. Apple, Jr., "McNamara Recalls, and Regrets, Vietnam," *New York Times*, April 9, 1995, page 1.

46. Frank J. Donner, *The Age of Surveillance* (New York: Alfred A. Knopf, 1980), page 183.

47. Charles Goodell, *Political Prisoners*, pages 90-91.

48. Frank J. Donner, *The Age of Surveillance*, pages 181-182. John T. Elliff, *The Reform of FBI Intelligence Operations* (Princeton: Princeton University Press, 1979), pages 128-129.

49. John T. Elliff, *The Reform*, pages 5 and 21.

50. Frank J. Donner, *The Age of Surveillance*, page 181.

51. John T. Elliff, *The Reform*, page 5. *Report of the Department of Justice Task Force to Review the FBI Martin Luther King, Jr., Security and Assassination Investigations.* Jan. 11, 1977, pages 1 and 123-149.

52. Sigmund Diamond, *Compromised Campus*, pages 278-279.

53. Frank J. Donner, *The Age of Surveillance*, page xii.

54. Frank J. Donner, *The Age of Surveillance*, page 4.

55. Frank J. Donner, *The Age of Surveillance*, pages 6-7.

56. Charles Goodell, *Political Prisoners*, page 255.

57. Albert Einstein, *Ideas and Opinions* (New York: Dell Publishing Co., 1973), pages 160 and 167.

58. Herbert Mitgang, *Dangerous Dossiers*, pages 263-265.

59. Eric Schmitt, "2 Submarine Makers Vie for a $60 Billion Project," *New York Times*, May 17, 1995, page 1.

CHAPTER 19: BUILDING A PUBLIC HEALTH SYSTEM

1. Barbara Tuchman, *A Distant Mirror: The Calamitous 14th Century* (New York: Ballantine Books, 1978), pages 93-94.

2. *Federalist*, No. 31.

3. Michael Kammen, *Mystic Chords of Memory: The Transformation of Tradition in American Culture* (New York: Alfred A. Knopf, 1991), page 571.

4. Robert Mehr and Emerson Cammack, *Principles of Insurance*, 7th ed. (Homewood, Illinois: Richard D. Irwin, Inc., 1980), pages 32-35.

5. Joseph D. Beasley, *The Betrayal of Health: The Impact of Nutrition, Environment, and Lifestyle on Illness in America* (New York: Times Books, 1991), pages 205-206.

6. John McDougall and Mary McDougall, *The McDougall Plan* (Clinton, New Jersey: New Win Publishing, 1983), page 183.

7. John McDougall and Mary McDougall, *The McDougall Plan*, page 184.

8. Marc Sorenson, *Mega Health* (Ivins, Utah: National Institute of Fitness, 1993), page 213.

9. Marc Sorenson, *Mega Health*, page 213.

10. Joseph D. Beasley, *The Betrayal of Health*, page 4.

11. Joseph D. Beasley, *The Betrayal of Health*, pages 99-132.

12. Joseph D. Beasley, *The Betrayal of Health*, pages 119 and 133-134.

13. Joseph D. Beasley, *The Betrayal of Health*, page 84.

14. Joseph D. Beasley, *The Betrayal of Health*, page 98.

15. Joseph D. Beasley, *The Betrayal of Health*, pages 20-21.

16. Joseph D. Beasley, *The Betrayal of Health*, page 16.

17. Joseph D. Beasley, *The Betrayal of Health*, page 139.

18. Joseph D. Beasley, *The Betrayal of Health*, pages 102 and 68.

19. Joseph D. Beasley, *The Betrayal of Health*, page 185.

20. Joseph D. Beasley, *The Betrayal of Health*, pages 173-174.

21. Joseph D. Beasley, *The Betrayal of Health*, page 102.

22. Joseph D. Beasley, *The Betrayal of Health*, page 132.

23. Joseph D. Beasley, *The Betrayal of Health*, page 208.

24. Joseph D. Beasley, *The Betrayal of Health*, page 208.

REFERENCES

25. Joseph D. Beasley, *The Betrayal of Health*, pages 101, 143-146, 28, and 49.

26. Joseph D. Beasley, *The Betrayal of Health*, page 200.

27. Joseph D. Beasley, *The Betrayal of Health*, pages 200-201.

28. Joseph D. Beasley, *The Betrayal of Health*, pages 151-152, 199, and 202.

29. Joseph D. Beasley, *The Betrayal of Health*, page 206.

30. Joseph D. Beasley, *The Betrayal of Health*, page 201.

31. Susan Edelman, "Hackensack Doctor's License Pulled: Put Patients at Risk, State Says," *The Record* (Bergen County, N. J.), Jan. 1, 1993, page 1.

32. J. Hector St. John de Crèvecoeur, *Letters from an American Farmer and Sketches of Eighteenth-Century America* (New York: Viking Penguin, Inc., 1986), page 150.

33. J. Hector St. John de Crèvecoeur, *Letters*, page 360.

34. J. Hector St. John de Crèvecoeur, *Letters*, pages 377-378.

35. Alexis de Tocqueville, *Democracy in America* (Garden City, New York: Doubleday and Co., 1969), pages 463 and 464.

36. Harris L. Coulter, *Divided Legacy: The Conflict Between Homeopathy and the American Medical Association* (Berkeley: North Atlantic Books, 1982), page 49.

37. Harris L. Coulter, *Divided Legacy*, pages 20, 39, and 53.

38. Harris L. Coulter, *Divided Legacy*, page 17.

39. Harris L. Coulter, *Divided Legacy*, page 17.

40. Harris L. Coulter, *Divided Legacy*, pages 39-40.

41. Harris L. Coulter, *Divided Legacy*, pages 94-99.

42. Harris L. Coulter, *Divided Legacy*, pages 442-450.

43. John Langone, *Chiropractors: A Consumer's Guide* (Reading, Mass.: Addison-Wesley Publishing Co., 1982), pages 77 and 37. Walter I. Wardwell, *Chiropractic: History and Evolution of a New Profession* (St. Louis: Mosby Year Book, 1992), pages 45, 174, and 285-286.

44. Robert S. Mendelsohn, *Confessions of a Medical Heretic* (Chicago: Contemporary Books, 1979), pages x-xi.

45. Robert S. Mendelsohn, *Confessions*, page 113.

46. Personal interview of Dr. Anthony Carusone on June 21, 1995.

47. Joseph D. Beasley, *The Betrayal of Health*, page 199.

48. Joseph D. Beasley, *The Betrayal of Health*, page 14.

49. Joseph D. Beasley, *The Betrayal of Health*, page 15.

50. Joseph D. Beasley, *The Betrayal of Health*, pages 101, 143-146, 28, and 49.

51. Joseph D. Beasley, *The Betrayal of Health*, page 194.

52. Joseph D. Beasley, *The Betrayal of Health*, page 210.

53. Joseph D. Beasley, *The Betrayal of Health*, page 211.

54. William Longgood, *The Poisons in Your Food* (New York: Simon and Schuster, 1960), page 185.

55. Joseph D. Beasley, *The Betrayal of Health*, pages 195-199.

56. Adelle Davis, *Let's Get Well* (New York: Harcourt, Brace and World, 1965), foreword by Joseph C. Risser, M. D., pages vii-ix.

57. René Dubos, *Mirage of Health* (New Brunswick, N. J.: Rutgers University Press, 1987), page 143.

58. Paul Brodeur, "Annals of Law: The Asbestos Industry on Trial," *New Yorker*, June 10, 1985, page 49, at page 50.

59. Paul Brodeur, "Annals of Law," page 79.

60. Paul Brodeur, "Annals of Law," pages 57-60.

61. Philip M. Boffey, "Dioxin Link Cited in Abnormalities," *New York Times*, April 18, 1986, page 13.

62. Marian Burros, "Residue of Chemicals in Meat Leads to Debate on Hazards," *New York Times*, March 15, 1983, page 1.

63. Philip Shabecoff, "Dioxin in Breast Milk is Evaluated in Private Study," *New York Times*, Dec. 18, 1987, page 1.

64. Gordon Bishop, "Report Says U. S. Could Take Lessons from Europe on Safe Trash Burning," *Star-Ledger* (Newark, N. J.), June 23, 1986, page 13.

65. Philip Shabecoff, "Dioxin in Breast Milk."

66. Marc Lappé, *Chemical Deception: The Toxic Threat to Health and the Environment* (San Francisco: Sierra Club Books, 1991), pages 9 and 125-148.

67. William Longgood, *The Poisons in Your Food* (New York: Simon and Schuster, 1960), page 118.

68. *Federalist*, No. 10.

69. William Greider, *Who Will Tell the People* (New York: Simon and Schuster, Touchstone Ed., 1993), pages 66 and 87-88.

70. Philip Shabecoff, "On the Move but Not Yet on the Wane: Toxic Wastes Go From One Leaky Dump to Another," *New York Times*, Nov. 18, 1984, section 4, page 2.

71. Robert Cohen, "GAO Sees Wider Toxic Waste Woes," *Star-Ledger* (Newark, N. J.), Jan. 15, 1988, page 35.

72. Mary Derine Worobee, *Toxic Substances Control Primer* (Washington, D. C.: The Bureau of National Affairs, Inc., 1984), pages 109-116.

73. Editorial, "Toxic Air and the E. P. A. Tortoise," *New York Times*, June 17, 1985, page 18.

74. Leo H. Carney, "The Environment: Sewage in the Ocean," *New York Times*, New Jersey Weekly Section, Sept. 22, 1985, page 24.

75. Kim Murphy, "Nation's New Toxic Pollution Threat: Runoff From City Streets," *Daily Journal* (Elizabeth, N. J.), Nov. 12, 1985, page 1.

76. Associated Press, Washington, D. C., "Report Says Yearly Health Cost Will Hit $1 Trillion," *Star-Ledger* (Newark, N. J.), Jan. 5, 1993, page 4.

77. Bob Herbert, "Buying Clothes Without Exploiting Children," *New York Times*, Aug. 4, 1995, page 27, op-ed.

CHAPTER 20: FOR LIBERALS AND CONSERVATIVES

1. *Encyclopaedia Britannica*, 15th ed., macropaedia, s.v. "liberalism."

2. *Encyclopaedia Britannica*, 15th ed., macropaedia, s.v. "conservatism."

3. Richard Cobb and Colin Jones, eds., *Voices of the French Revolution* (Topsfield, Mass.: Salem House Publishers, 1988), pages 102-103.

4. Stanley Ayling, *Edmund Burke: His Life and Opinions* (New York: St. Martin's Press, 1988), pages 80-81.

5. Russell Kirk, *The Conservative Mind: From Burke to Santayana* (Chicago: Henry Regnery Company, 1953), page 63.

6. Stanley Ayling, *Edmund Burke*, page 285.

7. *Encyclopaedia Britannica*, 15th ed., macropaedia, s.v. "conservatism."

8. David P. Barasch, *The L Word* (New York: William Morrow and Company, 1992), page 218.

9. David P. Barasch, *The L Word*, page 217.

10. Gordon K. Durnil, *The Making of a Conservative Environmentalist* (Bloomington, Ind.: Indiana University Press, 1995).

11. Gordon K. Durnil, *Conservative Environmentalist*, page 12.

12. Gordon K. Durnil, *Conservative Environmentalist*, page 12.

13. Gordon K. Durnil, *Conservative Environmentalist*, page ix.

14. Gordon K. Durnil, *Conservative Environmentalist*, page ix.

15. Gordon K. Durnil, *Conservative Environmentalist*, page 186.

16. Gordon K. Durnil, *Conservative Environmentalist*, page 21.

17. Gordon K. Durnil, *Conservative Environmentalist*, page 47.

18. Gordon K. Durnil, *Conservative Environmentalist*, pages 62 and 133-134.

19. Gordon K. Durnil, *Conservative Environmentalist*, page 164.

20. Gordon K. Durnil, *Conservative Environmentalist*, page 161.

21. Gordon K. Durnil, *Conservative Environmentalist*, page 128.

22. Gordon K. Durnil, *Conservative Environmentalist*, page 157.

23. Gordon K. Durnil, *Conservative Environmentalist*, pages 185 and 107.

24. Gordon K. Durnil, *Conservative Environmentalist*, page 185.

25. Gordon K. Durnil, *Conservative Environmentalist*, page 184.

26. Gordon K. Durnil, *Conservative Environmentalist*, page 165.

27. *Encyclopaedia Britannica*, 15th ed., macropaedia, s.v. "conservatism."

28. Adin Steinsaltz, *The Essential Talmud* (New York: Basic Books, Inc., 1976), pages 24-26.

29. *Encyclopaedia Britannica*, 15th ed., macropaedia, s.v. "Shammai."

30. Adin Steinsaltz, *The Essential Talmud*, pages 25-26. *Encyclopaedia Britannica*, 15th ed., macropaedia, s.v. "Hillel."

31. Adin Steinsaltz, *The Essential Talmud*, pages 6-7.

32. Joseph F. Sullivan, "Kean Rejects Race for Senate, Citing 'Mean Spirited G. O. P.,'" *New York Times*, Aug. 31, 1995, page B1.

33. Joseph D. Beasley, *The Betrayal of Health: The Impact of Nutrition, Environment, and Lifestyle on Illness in America* (New York: Times Books, 1991), page 98.

34. Barbara Tuchman, "A Nation in Decline," *New York Times Magazine*, Aug. 20, 1987, page 52.

35. Richard B. Morris, *Seven Who Shaped Our Destiny* (New York: Harper and Row, 1973), page 1.

REFERENCES

CHAPTER 21: ARTICLE FOUR MEETINGS

1. Theodore Roszak, *Unfinished Animal: The Aquarian Frontier and the Evolution of Consciousness* (New York: Harper and Row, 1975), page 3.

2. Theodore Roszak, *Unfinished Animal*, page 4.

3. René Dubos, *Mirage of Health, Utopias, Progress, and Biological Change* (New Brunswick, N. J.: Rutgers University Press, 1987), page 237.

4. Gary Null, *Nutrition and the Mind* (New York: Four Walls Eight Windows, 1995), pages 160-165.

5. Beatrice Trum Hunter, *Consumer Beware! Your Food and What's Been Done To It* (New York: Simon and Schuster, 1971), pages 211-217. Jane Heimlich, *What Your Doctor Won't Tell You* (New York: Harper Perennial, 1990), pages 96-97 and 100. David Steinman, *Diet For a Poisoned Planet* (New York: Harmony Books, 1990), pages 160-161.

6. Russell L. Blaylock, *Excitotoxins: The Taste That Kills* (Sante Fe, N. M.: Health Press, 1994).

7. Russell L. Blaylock, *Excitotoxins*, page xx.

8. Russell L. Blaylock, *Excitotoxins*, page xxii.

9. Russell L. Blaylock, *Excitotoxins*, pages 35-36.

10. Russell L. Blaylock, *Excitotoxins*, page 216.

11. Russell L. Blaylock, *Excitotoxins*, pages 33-35.

12. Russell L. Blaylock, *Excitotoxins*, pages 35-36.

13. Russell L. Blaylock, *Excitotoxins*, page 34.

14. H. J. Roberts, *Aspartame (NutraSweet®) Is It Safe?* (Philadelphia: The Charles Press, 1990).

15. H. J. Roberts, *Aspartame*, page 213.

16. H. J. Roberts, *Aspartame*, page 121.

17. Russell L. Blaylock, *Excitotoxins*, page 218. Marion Burros, "Eating Well: On Labeling for MSG and Poultry," *New York Times*, Oct. 18, 1995, page C4.

18. John Merrow, "Reading, Writing and Ritalin," *New York Times*, Oct. 21, 1995, page 21, op-ed.

19. Gary Wills, "The New Revolutionaries," *New York Review of Books*, Aug. 10, 1995, page 50.

20. David Sanger, "Real Politics: Why Suharto Is In and Castro Is Out," *New York Times*, Oct. 31, 1995, page 3.

21. Victor Arthur and Robert G. Arthur, "Still Toxic, After All These Years," *Natural Living Journal*, April, 1995, page 1.

CHAPTER 22: FULFILLING THE PROMISE

1. Wendell Berry, "A Defense of the Family Farm," page 164 and "Six Agricultural Fallacies," page 123 in *Home Economics: Fourteen Essays by Wendell Berry* (San Francisco: North Point Press, 1987).

2. Vance Packard, *The Waste Makers* (New York: David McKay Company, 1960), page 6.

3. Carl Sandburg, *Abraham Lincoln: The Prairie Years and the War Years* (New York: Galahad Books, 1993), pages 247-248.

4. Carl Sandburg, *Abraham Lincoln*, pages 357-359.

5. Carl Sandburg, *Abraham Lincoln*, page 23.

compiled by Marianne Williams

ABOUT THE AUTHOR

Michael Diamond studied political science and law at Rutgers University. He served as an enforcement administator and chief regulatory officer at the New Jersey Department of Environmental Protection. At present, Mr. Diamond practices law in Union, New Jersey. He has worked with a wide array of clients in the environmental field.

Mr. Diamond has made numerous presentations about the relationship between environmental threats and the United States Constitution. He has spoken at schools, to business organizations, and environmental groups. His writings on that topic have been widely circulated and well received.

PUBLICATION ORDERS

To purchase additional copies of *If You Can Keep It*, write, fax, or call

Brass Ring Press
P. O. Box 2697
251 North Ave. West
Westfield, NJ 07091

To order call toll free (800) 777-8145

telephone (908) 317-9300

fax (908) 232-6860

Include your name, mailing address, telephone number, credit card company, card number, expiration date, and the number of books you wish to receive.

If you prefer to pay by check, enclose a check or money order for $15.00 per book, plus $3.50 for shipping and handling of the first book. Add $0.50 to cover shipping and handling for each additional book in the same order. Make the check or money order payable to Brass Ring Press.

New Jersey residents are to add 6% sales tax ($0.90) for each book ordered.

ORGANIZING
ARTICLE FOUR MEETINGS

For more information about organizing Article Four meetings and action networks in your state, write to Michael Diamond, c/o Brass Ring Press, P. O. Box 2697, 251 North Ave. West, Westfield, NJ 07091.